RAIN OR SHINE

Walks in the Lake District
Whatever the Weather

ABOUT THE AUTHOR

Christopher Mitchell was born in Bridlington in 1949. He studied at the University of Hull, where he obtained an honours degree in Zoology and Psychology and was awarded an MSc for his research on insect behaviour.

He has worked as an Assistant Warden at Eskdale Youth Hostel and as an Assistant Instructor at the Eskdale Outward Bound Mountain School.

In 1979 he founded and directed the first private Field Study Centre on the Isle of Skye, where he has been leading field groups for over 20 years. Since 1990, he has been employed as an Auxiliary Weather Reporter for the Meteorological Office.

He is married with two children.

RAIN OR SHINE

Walks in The Lake District
Whatever the Weather

by
Christopher Mitchell

2 POLICE SQUARE, MILNTHORPE, CUMBRIA, LA7 7PY
www.cicerone.co.uk

ISBN 1 85284 334 6
© Christopher Mitchell 2002

Photographs: © Christopher Mitchell, unless otherwise indicated
Drawings: © Sarah Mitchell
Location Map: © Christopher Mitchell
Route Maps: by Christopher Mitchell, based on Ordnance Survey material by permission of Ordnance Survey on behalf of the Controller of Her Majesty's Stationery Office, © Crown Copyright MC 100036766.

DEDICATION

This book is dedicated to my wife, Janet.

Advice to Readers

Readers are advised that while every effort is taken by the author to ensure the accuracy of this guidebook, changes can occur which may affect the contents. It is advisable to check locally on transport, accommodation, shops, etc, but even rights of way can be altered.

The publisher would welcome notes of any such changes.

Front cover: Looking across to Ullswater from Moor Divock

CONTENTS

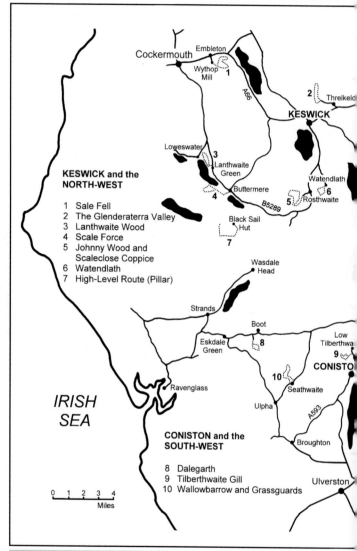

KESWICK and the NORTH-WEST

1 Sale Fell
2 The Glenderaterra Valley
3 Lanthwaite Wood
4 Scale Force
5 Johnny Wood and
  Scaleclose Coppice
6 Watendlath
7 High-Level Route (Pillar)

CONISTON and the SOUTH-WEST

8 Dalegarth
9 Tilberthwaite Gill
10 Wallowbarrow and Grassguards

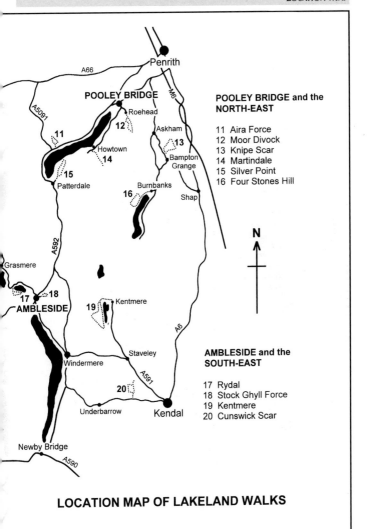

POOLEY BRIDGE and the
NORTH-EAST

11 Aira Force
12 Moor Divock
13 Knipe Scar
14 Martindale
15 Silver Point
16 Four Stones Hill

AMBLESIDE and the
SOUTH-EAST

17 Rydal
18 Stock Ghyll Force
19 Kentmere
20 Cunswick Scar

LOCATION MAP OF LAKELAND WALKS

PREFACE

There are hundreds of guidebooks on the Lake District but none of them deals specifically with the problem of where to walk and what to see in wet weather. The idea of writing such a guide suggested itself after a number of years leading field study groups on the Isle of Skye.

As in the Lake District, Skye has one of the highest annual rainfalls in the British Isles and is a magnet for hillwalkers and climbers. The problems are the same: what is there to look at when the mist comes down and you can't see further than the garden gate? How do you entertain a group of keen birdwatchers when it's been raining solidly for three days? Such problems constantly presented themselves over the years and, through necessity, a strategy evolved to deal with hill-walking in wet weather.

When visibility was low and the tops were out of bounds, I found myself looking at what was close to hand. As a field biologist, that meant looking for animal tracks and signs and focusing on wild flowers and the underlying rocks. But how do you salvage something from a wet, misty day in winter when the flowers have died back and the animals are all sensibly hiding from the weather – like *you* feel you should be!

With so little to work on, the mind is concentrated and the eyes are focused on the smallest detail. It meant a new way of looking at a familiar landscape and extracting information that was exciting enough to make the casual visitor forget the weather.

It wasn't good enough just to identify a rock or specific plant and give it its scientific name. What made it interesting was discovering how and why things were where they were. The walks became an exercise in looking for clues and solving mysteries. The emphasis was not on covering great distances but on enjoying the journey.

It is these same techniques, gathered from over 20 years of leading wet-weather walks on Skye, that are incorporated into this Lakeland guide. Twenty walks have been chosen to cover all regions of the Lake District so that you will be able to try them out wherever you happen to be when the weather closes in.

When I first began planning this book, I was a little uncertain as to which walks would 'work'. The walks had to be fairly short, averaging 2–3 miles/3–4.5km, with little strenuous climbing. They had to be mostly low-level and preferably with sheltered sections. And most important of all, each walk had to have at least two or three novel findings that would hold people's interest – something that was unexpected and that they hadn't seen before.

The 20 walks included in this book were chosen on this basis. There were some surprises. When the High-Level Route on Pillar was suggested for inclusion, most people thought it would be unsuitable. It turned out to be one of the most interesting walks in the book. And the Bronze Age artefacts on Moor Divock and Four Stones Hill were a revelation. Even those walks that I expected to be good on a wet day – such as Aira Force, Dalegarth and Scale Force – all produced the unexpected.

The 20 walks chosen are really just a sample of what there is to see in the Lake District in wet weather. Hopefully it will encourage the reader to revisit their own favourite haunts and see them in a new light... even in the rain!

Chris Mitchell
Isle of Skye
2001

PLEASE NOTE

Care should always be taken when walking in hill country, especially in wet weather. Where appropriate, attention has been drawn to specific matters of safety. The author and publisher cannot take responsibility for any accidents or injury incurred while following these walks.

Many of the features mentioned in this book are in Sites of Special Scientific Interest (SSSIs), Regionally Important Geological and Geomorphological Sites (RIGS) or are Scheduled Ancient Monuments. Please try and keep disturbance to a minimum and leave plants, rock faces and fossil sites as you found them for others to see.

The features mentioned in these walks will change naturally over time. If you think these changes should be included in the next edition, I should be most grateful if you would inform the publisher.

The route descriptions do not imply a right of way and, where necessary, permission to use footpaths should be sought.

ACKNOWLEDGEMENTS

First of all I would like to thank my wife Janet for her continued support throughout this project. I am especially grateful to Robert Arnold for introducing me to computer graphics which proved to be such a help in producing the detailed maps.

Thanks also to Ralph and Jane Blain at the 'Havelock' guesthouse in the Duddon Valley; Howard and Ruth Holden, formerly of Lambfoot House, Embleton; Jean Colston of Sunny Wood, Staveley, and Red and Pat Graham of Oakfields, Yanwath, for all their hospitality and help with the walks in their area; also the Warden of Longthwaite Youth Hostel for providing information on Johnny Wood and Scaleclose Coppice.

My special thanks go to Dr Alan Smith (General Secretary of the Cumberland Geological Society) for his help in identifying various geological samples and for trying to fill the many gaps in my geological knowledge.

Thanks also to Derrick Holdsworth (Cumbria measurer for the Tree Register of the British Isles) for his extensive contribution to the Aira Force walk; Mrs Edna Smith and her colleagues at the Natural History Museum for advice and help on various obscure algae, and Geoff Collins (formerly Head Gardener at Inverewe) who spent many hours helping me with plant identification.

Anne Rowe and her colleagues at the Cumbria Record Office in Kendal and the staff at Ambleside's Armitt Museum and Library were most helpful in finding numerous historical references, and Bette Hopkins (Cumbria Sites and Monuments Record Officer) deserves a special mention for patiently sifting through her records on Bronze Age sites in response to my many telephone enquiries.

John Hodgson (National Park Archaeologist) provided information on various archaeological sites; David Clarke and colleagues at Tullie House Museum helped with references on flora and fauna of the Borrowdale Woods and with information on dragonfly distribution; Dr Geoffrey Halliday (BSBI Recorder for Westmorland and Furness, and Cumberland), Andrew Currie and Dr Peter Holland helped with identifying difficult plants, whilst Dr Fred Slater of Cardiff University and Dr Tony Edwards of the Macaulay Land Use Research Institute gave me advice on wetland ecology.

I should also like to thank Dr Tony Cooper of the British Geological Survey for supplying information on graptolytes and the Skiddaw Slates and Mike Smith for the historical information on Martindale Old Church. Neil Robinson (Cumbria Naturalists Union) provided information on ant distribution and Roger Putnam (formerly Warden at Eskdale OBMS) helped me with some of the details on the Dalegarth walk. Special thanks go to Brad and Jean for helping out with transport on several occasions and to Jed and Helen for help with the computer. Thanks also to Peter and Helen Thompson and Phil and Heather Lyon who kindly agreed to check over and walk particular routes.

Finally, I should especially like to thank my daughter Sarah for providing the excellent pen-and-ink drawings that accompany and illuminate the text.

Symbol	Description	Symbol	Description
✚	Church		Lake Shoreline
◆	Buildings		Tarn
ℝ	Refreshments	~	River
ⓣ	Telephone		Stream (with waterfall)
ⓦⓒ	Public Toilets		Bridge
ⓟ	Public Car Park	:	Gate
❺	Site Number	○	Stile
	Crags		Wall (with gate)
	Scree		Fence (with stile)
*	Archaeological Feature		Road
	Deciduous Trees	-------	Track
			Route
	Coniferous Trees	------	Other Paths
		[	Seat

MAP KEY

INTRODUCTION

This is not a book for the faint-hearted: more for the desperate! I assume things are pretty bad – it's your main holiday, you've planned a week's walking in the hills and you thought you were prepared. You've packed the sun block (factor 15 at least), shorts, sun hat, designer shades, plenty of film in the camera – and it was great weather travelling to get here (what a sunset over Blencathra!). And now you're in Keswick and it's early morning and just look at it! Can't see the tops. Driving rain and it's blowing a gale.

Well, you've got this far and you've bought the book, so fear not – help is at hand.

First of all, it's a question of attitude. We British are pretty good at putting up with things. Bill Bryson remarked on a typically British catchphrase: 'Mustn't grumble!'

Well, of course you're going to grumble – it's been pouring down now for the past 12 hours and it's your holiday and why didn't we go to Sardinia anyway?

But relax. From now on things can only get better…

EQUIPMENT

What to Wear. As a hillwalker you are likely to be familiar with the latest hi-tech gear designed to protect you from the wind and rain. There is a mass of information on clothing design and fabrics and most walking magazines have test-reports on all the latest models. What I should like to mention here are some personal observations that I have found useful when facing wet weather.

First, if like me you wear spectacles, you will have trouble in the rain and particularly in fine drizzle and mist. Coating the lenses with a thin layer of washing-up liquid before setting off is supposed to help a little. But I have found the simplest protection is to wear a broad-rimmed trilby-style hat pulled down low under the jacket hood. A base-ball hat is a reasonable alternative but will not give quite as much protection. A handful of tissues are useful for wiping the lenses, but make sure they are kept dry inside a plastic bag.

In excessively wet weather, the weak spot in your clothing will be around the shoulders and neck and, whatever type of jacket you wear, this is where you will feel the wet first. One way of combatting this is to wear a small cotton towel like a scarf to absorb what gets through.

If it gets really windy and your hood has a loose draw-cord adjuster, it can get annoying (and dangerous) if it starts whipping about around your face. The problem is solved by zipping the ends inside the jacket or into the breast pockets, if you have them.

If it isn't windy and you are walking low down in the valley with no fear of falling over dangerous ground and the rain is coming straight down – use an umbrella. Buy one that is a reasonable size, like a golf umbrella. It should be stronger than the town varieties, but even so, if the wind gets up, beware! – *only use it on safe, low-valley routes*, not where you could be blown off balance. When it's not in use it can be strapped to the rucksack like an ice-axe.

Footwear should suit the type of terrain. On the high fells, good-quality boots are standard. Various manufacturers have now produced socks that are 100 per cent waterproof and breathable. They are expensive but they will upgrade an old pair of leaky boots. They will also transform a pair of fell-running shoes, although care is needed when walking through sharp undergrowth such as gorse or brambles to avoid puncturing the built-in membrane. On low-level ground without any rock hazards, 'wellies' will guarantee you dry feet.

The Midge Problem. Midges can be a real problem from June to September when the wind drops below 5mph and you find yourself in woodland, wet moorland or bracken. The situation is made worse when it is humid or there is fine drizzle. The most effective chemical defence is DEET (diethytoluamide) but this is a very unpleasant chemical in the concentrations that need to be used.

Once you are aware that midges are present, your nervous system will become sensitised so that anything lightly touching the skin will be interpreted as a biting midge. A bit of self-hypnosis may help you.

There are some very effective midge-hoods or, if you don't mind looking like a bank-robber, a pair of nylon tights will help, especially if pulled over a broad-rimmed hat.

Photography. Taking photographs in wet weather has its own problems. The standard advice is to use a fast film (200 ASA or above) for low light levels. If you have a camera with slow shutter speeds, you could experiment and go for high quality using 50 ASA film, but you will need a tripod and a cable-release to keep things steady. A slow film will also enable you to capture waterfalls using a slow shutter speed to give a soft appearance to moving water.

When photographing weather phenomena with 35mm film, you will need a wide-angle lens to capture a complete rainbow or the halos around the sun. To increase the contrast of cloud formations use a polarising filter.

WEATHER

Cloud Types. In official MET Office jargon, rain comes out of low and medium-level clouds (stratus, stratocumulus or nimbostratus). Showers and thunderstorms come from low-level cloud (cumulus and cumulonimbus); if you're in drizzle, you're in plain simple stratus.

The shape of the cloud will tell you what the air is doing: whether it is rising, rippling along gently, or pressing down violently. Some of the most interesting clouds are associated with cliffs, mountains and hills and are known as *orographic* or wave clouds. These reveal the flow of air moving over land forms. Stacks of 'dinner plates', 'flying saucers', 'almonds' and fish-shapes show that the wind has been deflected into regular waves. The cloud condenses in those sections of the wave that are rising and will appear stationary over the ground that is causing it.

Examples are seen in the north Pennines when a steady north-easterly air-flow produces the 'Helm Bar' on Crossfell. The surface waves produced by the intercepting line of hills are compressed underneath a layer of warmer air at a specific height above the ridge. The wind is called the 'Helm Wind' and its force can be felt as far west as Coniston where it funnels through the gap of Walna Sca Road.

In the Lake District itself, wave clouds are more likely to appear after a prolonged spell of cold, dry, easterly winds when regular stationary waves are shown by patterns in the higher clouds. But it's the wet, westerly air from across the Atlantic that concerns us here. This can produce low-level orographic clouds on those west-facing hills and cliff faces that first intercept it. Keep a look-out over Buttermere, Wastwater and Eskdale for cottonwool-like shrouds covering the peaks and ridges. This indicates very moist air and is the start of stratus cloud leading to drizzle.

Wave clouds – often a result of dry, easterly winds

Downward movement of air is seen in certain cumulonimbus clouds and indicates violent showers of rain or hail with possible thunderstorms. The tell-tale sign is the formation of dark udder-like bulges rapidly forming and changing on the cloud's undersurface. The technical term is *mamma* (because of their shape) – but there's nothing comforting when these appear.

Lightning. Electric storms may be a dramatic sight but they can be a frightening and dangerous experience if you happen to be caught out on a summit ridge. This happened to me on the top of Knipe Scar and my first reaction was to throw away my metal-tipped umbrella and to shelter under the limestone cliff. The modern consensus would indicate that I was right to discard the umbrella but wrong to shelter under a cliff where the currents could jump across the 'spark-gap'.

The best current advice is to get off the summit peak or ridge if possible and find an area of broken scree out in the open. Take up a crouched position sitting on top of your rucksack and keep your hands on your lap and away from the ground.

Avoid sheltering under a tree, particularly if it is tall and isolated. A cave may provide safe shelter, provided that there is a minimum of 10ft/3m head room and a gap of 3ft/1m between you and the side walls.

Brocken Spectre. In certain conditions, when clouds are trapped in the valleys and the tops are in sunshine, your shadow can be cast onto the mist to form what is known as a brocken spectre (named after its frequent occurrence on the Brocken ridge in Germany). A halo or 'glory' is seen around the head formed on the same principle as a rainbow.

Rainbows. The typical rainbow is known as a 'primary bow'. If a 'secondary bow' occurs, it is wider and fainter and separated from the inner bow by a dark area of sky. There is also a 'reflective bow' reflected more or less straight upwards from the surface of a lake where the normal rainbow meets the surface. Yet another variation can be seen when standing on a ridge or summit pinnacle, with a rain shower sweeping below into the valley – the rainbow may then become a complete circle.

The colours of the rainbow depend on the size of the raindrops. If the drop diameter is greater than 1mm, there will be a strong red band. If the drop size is reduced to 0.3mm, red disappears leaving orange as the first band. When the water droplets approach 0.05mm, a white 'fogbow' appears.

Halos. Halos around the sun or moon are often a sign of wet weather ahead. When there are no complicating atmospheric factors, the first indication of an approaching 'low' are the ice crystals of high altitude cirrostratus forming a 22-degree halo. Depending on the conditions, various other optical effects can be seen including 'mock suns'. As the cloud level drops, the sun appears as if through frosted glass (thin altostratus) before disappearing as the altostratus thickens, and rain is only a matter of hours away.

USING THE MAPS

This is not an ordinary guidebook. The routes do not lead directly to the summit ridges or cover great distances. They wander slowly from boulder to boulder, or from tree to tree. The walks may not be physically demanding but they do require concentration and careful map reading.

Each walk is described with the aid of a large-scale map and a detailed route description. In addition to the site numbers (see below), key place names and features from the maps are printed in bold type in the route description to aid orientation. It is recommended that both map and route details are studied carefully before setting out. The general Map Key is for use with all 20 route maps. Please note that where a gate and a stile occur side by side, only the stile is shown on the map and referred to in the text.

The routes have been marked by a thick line of dashes. *This does not reflect the nature of the path. In most instances the path is wide and obvious but there are some sections where there is no clear path to follow.*

Site numbers represent sites of significant interest: a place to stop and examine a particular rock, plant or landscape feature... or perhaps some animal tracks and signs. The things you will encounter at each site are described fully in the route description and you will find the site number printed in bold type, e.g. **site 5**, for easy reference. A shortened description can be found alongside each map in the form of a Site Summary which can be used if necessary as a quick reminder of what you will find at each numbered site. It has been arranged so that if it is raining heavily, the book can be carried open inside a clear plastic bag with the map and Site Summary side by side. This allows for quick and easy reference whilst on the move.

It is essential to familiarise yourself with the scale of *each* map before setting out – otherwise you may find yourself walking off the edge of the page in the first few minutes! If all 20 walks were laid out end to end, they would barely cover 60 miles/95km. Jos Naylor, the fell-running shepherd of Wasdale, would probably complete them all in under six hours!

Most hillwalkers are used to walking at 3 miles (4.5km) per hour with half an hour added for every 1000ft/300m of height gained (Naismith's formula). But to see these walks at their best, it is recommended that you average 1 mile (1.5km) per hour which means taking at least half a day to complete the longer routes. At this speed, hillwalking changes from being a physical exercise and becomes a forensic science!

In Keswick, waiting for Skiddaw to clear

At 1 mile per hour and with frequent stops you begin to see things in a different way. That boulder you are dejectedly sheltering under has its own story to tell. Did you know, for instance, that it is used

LICHEN CHECKLIST

The following list provides the 'common names' (where available) and the 'scientific names' of those lichens mentioned on the walks.

Crottle; *Parmelia saxatilis*.

Cup lichen; certain species of *Cladonia* with cup-like structures (for simplicity, I have also included those lichens that resemble matchsticks within this broad group).

Dog lichen; *Peltigera canina, P. polydactyla, P. horizontalis*.

Map lichen; *Rhizocarpon geographicum*.

Rock tripe; *Umbilicaria pustulata*.

Mustard-colour on bird perches (acid rock); *Candelariella vitellina*.

Yellow on bird perches (limestone); *Xanthoria parietina*.

Miniature 'trees' amongst heather; *Cladonia arbuscula* and *C. impexa*.

frequently by the Herdwick sheep as a rubbing-post, that it fell down from the rock face behind you between 10 and 15 years ago, and is a favourite perch for wheatears, a bird that migrates here from Africa each spring? It's all in the lichen, and its secrets are just waiting to be revealed...

Walk 1

SALE FELL

For those locked in with the crowds of Keswick on a wet day waiting for Skiddaw to clear, Sale Fell offers a way out. It's not far down the road and the bus will take you to Embleton.

There is an airiness about this part of Lakeland which contrasts with the claustrophobic atmosphere of Borrowdale. Perhaps it is because you are on the edge and able to look in at all your old favourite fells from a new perspective. Perhaps it is the chance to look out across the wide expanse of coastal plain to the sea. Up here you feel the wind in your face and it is a sea breeze.

It is difficult in such bracing conditions to walk slowly. The summit has a gentle gradient covered in short springy turf. On a clear day you can see across to Scotland.

When the mist comes down, the interest is maintained by the three distinct rock formations close to the summit cairn. Wainwright mentions them as being geologically significant, but he comes away in some confusion after trying to fathom out exactly what geologists have to say (see Wainwright's comment on John Postlethwaite in The North Western Fells; Sale Fell, 11). *On this walk, we will focus on the mysterious geology of Sale Fell's summit – and hope to find the exact whereabouts of the 'beautiful rock' quoted in A.W.'s description.*

THE ROUTE

From **Wythop Mill** the public road leads to a gate (sign: Kelswick Farm). Follow the farm road to the farm noting the white vein of quartz breaking through the shattered rock face of Dodd Crag above the bracken on your left. Below the quartz, the rock has been turned over on itself showing the extraordinary folding that led to the formation of Sale Fell (geologists call this the 'Sale Fell–Ling Fell Anticline').

CHECKLIST

Distance:	3.2 miles/5.2km.
Ascent:	650ft/200m.
Approximate Time:	3 hours.
Maps:	1:25 000 OS Outdoor Leisure 4, The English Lakes, North Western area. 1:50 000 OS Landranger 89 or 90. 1:25 000 British Geological Survey, Special Sheet NY 12, Lorton and Loweswater (S&D) 1990.
Terrain:	Dry underfoot for most of the way except for occasional muddy sections through Chapel Wood.
Degree of Shelter:	Very sheltered from strong winds and rain inside Chapel Wood. Can be exposed on the remaining sections particularly if the wind is coming from the south-west.
Stiles:	One (optional, alongside gate).
Special Considerations:	Please avoid damaging the rock outcrops on the summit of Sale Fell particularly when searching for graptolytes. Fossils may be found by examining loose stones with weathered faces without having to expose fresh surfaces.
Footwear:	Boots.
Parking:	There is a small lay-by (NY185293) in front of the gate leading to the Kelswick farm road with space for three or four cars. Wythop Mill village has only limited parking space and has no refreshments or public toilets. Far better to leave the car in Keswick and catch the bus to Embleton. The Wheatsheaf Inn provides lunch-time bar meals.
Public Transport:	Buses to Embleton stop outside the Wheatsheaf Inn (Stagecoach; service X4 and X5 every hour from Keswick to Cockermouth).

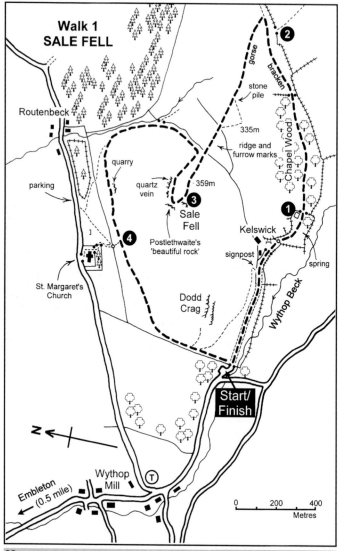

Walk 1
SALE FELL

gorse

bracken

stone
pile

335m

ridge and
furrow marks

Routenbeck

quarry

quartz
vein

359m

Sale
Fell

Chapel Wood

parking

Postlethwaite's
'beautiful rock'

Kelswick

signpost

spring

St. Margaret's
Church

Dodd
Crag

Wythop Beck

Start/
Finish

Z

Wythop
Mill

(T)

Embleton
(0.5 mile)

0   200   400
Metres

SALE FELL
SITE SUMMARY

1. **Ruins of Wythop Old Church (NY194291)**
   Plaques and information sheet showing history of this
   demolished church. Chapel Wood contains sessile oak and
   pied-flycatchers.

2. **Line of 'flag trees' (NY203294)**
   Old field-boundary showing effects of south-westerlies.
   Distinct zones of bracken and gorse caused by increasing
   wind exposure with altitude.

3. **Sale Fell summit (NY194297)**
   Fossil graptolytes trapped within 500 million year old
   mudstone. A rare intrusion of pink volcanic rock known as
   kersatite. An exposure of white quartz showing direction of
   Sale Fell-Ling Fell Anticline.

4. **Path junction (NY191300)**
   Alternative route back to Wythop Mill visiting St Margaret's
   Church. A stone lintel from the Old Church is on display
   inside.

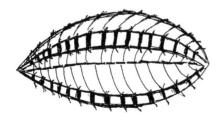

*Fossil graptolyte
(Pseudophyllograptus)
found on Sale Fell*

Inside the ruins of Wythop Old Church

As you stand here facing north-east, looking along the spine of these hills, imagine looking along a carpet that has been pushed sideways along its left-hand edge to form a 'ruckle' down the middle. This one-sided pressure then continued to push the fold over on itself.

Just before the farm buildings, you pass a turn-off on the left with a **signpost**: 'Public Footpath Wythop Church'. Do not take this path but continue on the farm road, past the farm buildings on your left. Cross the fence at the stile (or gate) which leads onto a pleasant grassy terrace.

You are about to enter **Chapel Wood** – an ancient sessile oak woodland that takes its name from the site of the old Wythop Church (**site 1**). Some of the church walls still remain. Here you will find a plaque and an information sheet with a photograph and a brief history of the building.

There is some uncertainty about when the church was built but there are records going back to the 16th Century. It was demolished in 1865 and a lintel with the date 1673 can be seen inside the new Wythop Church of St Margaret. It is thought that the bell was hung from one of the horizontal oak branches that can be found nearby. Some of the white quartz from the vein on Dodd Crag was used in the building and a piece remains on top of one of the ruined walls.

The path goes through a gate in a deer fence that encloses most of the woodland. After passing a small quarry on the left, look for nest boxes fixed to the trees all along the right-hand side of the path. They have been put here to encourage pied-flycatchers. Around the base of the oaks, you may see tiny clusters of the white-flowering heath bedstraw.

The narrow muddy path climbs gently through the wood until you reach a gate that brings you out onto open fellside. If the weather is clear, there are good views to the south of Broom Fell and Lord's Seat with Skiddaw out to the east.

The path follows a wire fence on the right. The fence makes a dog-leg bend to the right around a coppiced hazel and a hawthorn. After about 500ft/150m the fence makes a return dog-leg towards the path. Notice the corner-post. It serves as a rubbing-post for the local sheep and has been worn smooth on the side facing you. If you look over the fence at this point, the grass field shows signs of 'ridge and furrow' markings. It is difficult to give these markings a precise date. Some were made during the early medieval period (11th to 12th Century). Others, particularly those on the higher fell sides, are thought to date from the Napoleonic Wars when marginal land was cultivated to boost the country's food production.

After skirting above a boggy area alongside a short section of stone wall, you arrive at a gate (**site 2**). An ancient pathway can be seen winding its way across the field. The line taken follows an old field-boundary that would once have supported a stock-proof hedge. Now that the fields have been enlarged, the only sign of the former boundary is a line of straggly hawthorns. The branches of these old trees are being pulled constantly in one direction by the prevailing south-westerly winds. When trees produce this characteristic lop-sided growth, they are often known as 'flag trees'.

The wind direction also affects the shape of the trunk. Logs cut from a tree that has grown in sheltered conditions will usually be round. But if the tree has been wind-blown from one direction, the logs will be oval because of the extra growth that has been added in response to the bending forces.

Wind speed increases as you travel up a mountainside and the vegetation will often show this. Notice how the lower slopes of Sale Fell are covered in bracken but as you cross the 260m contour-line this is replaced by the more wind-resistant gorse. It is also interesting to

Gorse growing above the 250m contour-line on Sale Fell – one of the few shrubs that can resist sheep and strong winds

consider why these two different plants have continued to survive in an area grazed heavily by sheep. Gorse has a physical defence of sharp spines whereas bracken uses a more subtle chemical warfare. From March until August, the bracken's green leaves produce cyanide, whilst from September onwards, the cyanide disappears to be replaced by tannic acid – and the plant is left well alone.

Approximately 160ft/50m further along from site 2, the route leaves the main path and cuts back up the slope to your left (take care at this point – the junction can be difficult to find). The narrow path climbs steadily up the side of Sale Fell between extensive patches of **gorse**.

On reaching a shallow col and after passing a loose **pile of quarried stones**, the path forks. Keep to the right and aim for a gap in a low broken-down wall. Once through the gap, the path crosses a series of **ridge and furrow marks**. It then crosses a gap in a well-kept wall and climbs gently to the summit of Sale Fell.

Immediately north of the summit the land drops into a shallow corridor running approximately east–west. This is the direction of a vein of quartz some of which is visible 330ft/100m due north of the summit cairn. This vein of white quartz is one of many that run in a north-east to south-west direction along the anticline from Sale Fell across to Ling Fell.

From the summit of **Sale Fell**, take the grassy path heading west for 330ft/100m until you reach a harbour-like wall of rock with loose flaky slabs of stone scattered at its base (**site 3**). This is where geologists begin to get excited. We are standing on what used to be called 'Skiddaw Slate' (now called the 'Skiddaw Group' rocks). This is sedimentary rock deposited in the sea nearly 500 million years ago making it the oldest rock in the Lake District. It was formed from various combinations of mud, silt and sand and within it are trapped very small fossils known as graptolytes. They are some of the most primitive life-forms that can be linked with those animals that went on to develop backbones. You are not going to find a *T. rex* here. Instead, look on the flat surfaces of the weathered rocks for what look like delicate pencil marks about 4cm long. In fact these fossils were originally known as 'grapholites' from the Greek word *graphos* meaning something that has been written. The particular species found here is more easily spotted on flat weathered surfaces, where it displays a white crusty feather-like pattern. Like most delicate fossils, it is easier to see when the rock is wet.

From this fossil site, head north-west for a further 65ft/20m until you reach an outcrop on the edge of the summit plateau. This is **John Postlethwaite's 'beautiful rock'** mentioned in Wainwright's description of Sale Fell's summit. This volcanic rock intruded into the Skiddaw Group at a later date (about 400 million years ago). Postlethwaite called it 'minette' but more recent geological surveys refer to it as 'kersatite'. It is coloured pink because it contains a high proportion of feldspar.

Look carefully at the large boulders. On one of the vertical flat surfaces facing north, someone has carved a name and a date. The weathering makes it difficult to see, but if the light is right it seems to read: GLEN 1941.

Perhaps these unusual rocks were chosen as a final resting-place for someone's pet dog.

Before leaving the summit, walk east along the grassy corridor to examine the **quartz vein** and then retrace your steps back to the gap in the top wall.

Turn left at the wall until you reach a gate. Turn left again and follow the path as it keeps above the beck. Along this section, the path is a pleasant grassy terrace with good views over Bassenthwaite. The route now contours around the north flank of Sale Fell. Look carefully for a fork in the path and take the narrow stony path that bears left without losing height (the right-hand fork is wide and grassy and drops down to a gap in the wall below). This difficult section leads across to a small **quarry** with a white cross painted on one of its rocks (local enquiries have been unable to discover why this cross was painted here).

The path now becomes wide and grassy once again as it crosses the north-west side of Sale Fell. At first some height is lost as you drop down to a junction (**site 4**) where a path leads down to the 'new' church. For those who do not need to return to their car at the starting point, this provides an alternative route back to Wythop Mill following the narrow road from Routenhead. If you do visit the church, look inside the porch where you will find a stone lintel from the 'old' church with the date 1570 carved upon it.

To return to your starting point, continue from the junction at site 4 climbing steadily for the next 1300ft/400m. Eventually the path reaches the stone boundary wall that cuts across the west flank of Sale Fell and follows it closely, dropping steeply down to the starting point at the farm road gate.

Walk 2

THE GLENDERATERRA VALLEY

Northern Lakeland is characterised by massive deposits of marine sediments known as the Skiddaw Group rocks. The smooth outline and whale-back ridges covered in purple heather reflect an underlying structure that is rather regular. Some might call it rather dull compared with the fireworks of the central volcanic landscape.

If there has been pyrotechnics here, it has all been going on quietly underground. A mass of molten rock known as the Skiddaw Granite found its way into the mudstone and changed it. As the temperature dropped, mineral deposits were formed in fractures and cavities. The centre of this activity was an area north of the Glenderaterra Valley, once well known for its copper and lead mines.

On this walk, the granite centre is approached along the miners' track. Most of the geological events may have happened below ground but there are places where it shows itself on the surface. As you walk up the valley towards this former underground heat-source, you can see the rocks change beneath your feet. In places the dull mudstone gives way to spectacular crystal patterns. The rocks not only change colour – they even sound different!

THE ROUTE

From the car park above the **Blencathra Centre**, follow the miners' track that leads north-west past a small plantation of larch. The ground is regular and the gradient gentle all the way along the west flank of Blease Fell. The colour of the path is blue-grey. You are walking on mudstones that have remained more or less unchanged since they were deposited in deep water about 480 million years ago.

As you continue to climb, the path changes. At the level of the disused **concrete reservoirs** across to your left, flecks of white start to appear and as you approach the first gill, there are fragments that are coloured bright red and purple.

The path drops down to cross the beck and climbs up the other side, close to a bank of red scree (**site 1**). The colours reflect the iron in the rock and the chemistry is similar to what happens when iron-glazed pottery is fired in a kiln. High levels of oxygen during the firing-process produce red; low levels produce purple.

Look closely at some of the larger fragments. They are shot-through with spectacular patterns of white crystal. When viewed end-on with a microscope they are seen to contain dark cross-shaped inclusions giving them the name chiastolite (from the Greek word *khiasmos*, meaning cross).

Before leaving the gill, follow the beck upwards along its north side and then cross back over to the other bank to see the waterfall. The arrangement of crags on this right-hand side has kept a small area free of sheep. Underneath a rowan tree there is what could be regarded as a natural experiment – showing what can grow in this part of Lakeland when the ground is left ungrazed. Notice the tall growths of heather (*Calluna vulgaris*), woodrush and hard fern. There is also bilberry, but here it is left complete with all its berries.

Retrace your steps back to the miners' track. In a short distance you pass some very **tall rushes** (*Juncus effusus*) before crossing a small stream. About 115ft/35m past this stream on the left is a prominent **boulder**. Whenever I see one of these isolated rocks, I feel like a detective looking for clues. Notice the mustard-coloured lichen on top (a sign of perching birds); the polished vertical edge; the grass worn away below in a muddy depression; and the red stains – from the dye painted on the sheep that come here to rub themselves.

The path continues past some more unusually tall rushes before dropping down to the stone-slab footbridge crossing **Roughten Gill** (**site 2**). You are now much closer to the centre of the granite intrusion and the increased temperature has baked the local mudstone changing it into what geologists call 'hornfels'. The stone slabs that make up the bridge are good examples. Their altered crystal structure makes them hard and brittle, with a resonance similar to cast iron.

After crossing the bridge, look for a rock 33ft/10m ahead and to the right of the path. This rock shows all the signs of having an interesting geology – it is covered in geologists' hammer marks! The reason for the attention is that this particular hornfeld is speckled with black spots – the tell-tale sign of being heated by the underground granite.

The path passes by a stone ruin on the left before reaching another

CHECKLIST

Distance:	3.6 miles/5.8km.
Ascent:	500ft/150m.
Approximate Time:	3 to 4 hours.
Maps:	1:25 000 OS Outdoor Leisure 4, The English Lakes, North Western area; 1:50 000 OS Landranger 89 or 90; 1:50 000 British Geological Survey, England and Wales Sheet 29, Keswick.
Terrain:	The miners' tracks have good surfaces with easy gradients. NB. There is no clear path between sites 3 and 7.
Degree of Shelter:	A low-level route but with little shelter from strong winds.
Stiles:	Two (optional, alongside gates).
Special Considerations:	After a spell of prolonged rain, the river crossings may be difficult.
Footwear:	Boots.
Parking:	Blease Road end above Blencathra Centre (NY303257).
Public Transport:	Buses to Threlkeld, 1.5 miles/2.5km from Blencathra Centre (Stagecoach; services 73, 73A, X4 and X5). At least one bus every 2 hours most days leaves from Keswick.

ruin further ahead on the right (**site 3**). Although the roof has long gone, this is a good place to shelter and have lunch if the rain is blowing across horizontally.

These isolated walls are worth exploring in detail. As you stand facing the entrance, begin an anti-clockwise circuit by examining the rocks low down and to your right. Here you will find more hornfels with black spots. Coincidentally, these black-spotted rocks have black-spotted lichens on their surface.

Turn the first corner and make your way down the side to the south-

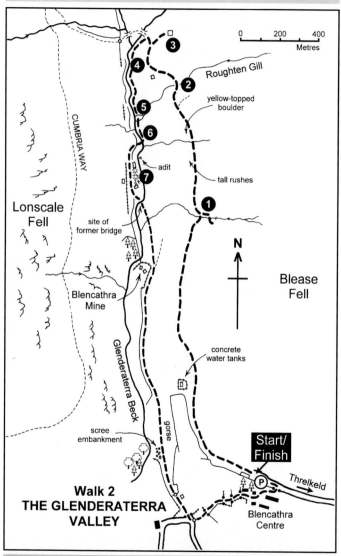

Walk 2
THE GLENDERATERRA
VALLEY

Flag trees alongside ancient field boundary at site 2, Sale Fell (Walk 1)

Grasmoor from Lanthwaite Wood across Lanthwaite Green (Walk 3)

Below High Doat looking over the pool to the Stonethwaite valley (Walk 5)

THE GLENDERATERRA VALLEY
SITE SUMMARY

1. **Gill and waterfall (NY299270)**
   Red metamorphic rock containing patterns of white crystal.

2. **Stone-slab footbridge (NY298276)**
   Bridge made of hornfels (from baked mudstone). Black speckling of rocks indicate nearby underground heat-source.

3. **Stone ruin (NY298278)**
   Walls covered in a variety of lichen including rock tripe.

4. **Collapsed adit (NY296277)**
   Stone-lined tunnel with quartz fragments. Eyebright growing on spoil-heap.

5. **Stream junction (NY296275)**
   Blocked adit and spoil-heaps. Fragments of white quartz, green malachite and yellow copper pyrite.

6. **Collapsed adit (NY297274)**
   Tunnel entrance with iron-stained quartz.

7. **The Glenderaterra Mine (NY297271)**
   Abandoned lead mine (Danger! Flooded vertical shafts). Large spoil-heaps still bare of plantlife after 100 years of weathering.

east corner. On top is the familiar yellow lichen, encouraged by the bird-droppings. Outside of this is that other sign of nitrogen – rock tripe (*Umbilicaria pustulata*). The Latin name reflects how it is attached to the rock and also describes the plant's surface which is covered in hollow pustules.

From this south-east corner, turn left to follow the back wall. Notice the two white rocks built into the wall approximately 3ft/1m above the ground. This is the Skiddaw Granite (found nearby in Sinen Gill) that produced the high temperatures and the consequent changes in the rocks that we have been seeing throughout this walk.

Follow the path as far as the next footbridge but do not cross it. Instead, drop down left from the path and follow the course of Sinen Gill. The path along this section is indistinct and boggy. Where the beck bends to the right there is a large boulder in the middle of the stream-bed. Several metres further, the boggy path goes alongside a ridge of spoil covered in fragments of quartz. You are now at **site 4**, which is the upper adit (horizontal entrance) of the old Glenderaterra Mine, later renamed the Brundholme Mine.

Just to the left of the spoil-heap there is a collapsed tunnel entrance. One section is still intact and acts as a narrow grassy bridge across the sunken channel. The remaining masonry shows how skillfully these tunnels were made, lined with dressed stone to form an arched roof. As you look inside facing the tunnel entrance, a large yellow-stained rock can be seen on the left-hand side. This is 'gossan', a type of iron-rich quartz that was a signal to miners that other minerals could be present and may have weathered out nearby.

Before leaving this ridge of spoil, see if you can spot the tiny, white-flowering eyebright. The name comes from its shape which resembles an eye complete with eyelash. This plant was one of the classic herbal remedies for eye problems, an example of the so-called 'Doctrine of Signatures': like cures like.

The path continues along the left bank of what is now Glenderaterra Beck. On your left is a mossy area with sphagnum and sundew. Ahead of you are two streams where Roughten Gill forms a junction with the beck (**site 5**). Before reaching the first stream, there is another blocked adit high up on your left side. The spoil-heap is overgrown but once again there are small fragments of quartz crystals on the surface. Look carefully in front of the first stream amongst a flat area of gravel. Here you will find small fragments (less than 1cm long) of the vivid green copper ore known as 'malachite' together with brassy yellow copper pyrites: the copper equivalent of fool's gold.

Cross the two streams (the second stream is quite difficult to cross and after heavy rain you may have to accept getting wet feet at this point). Continue along the east side of Glenderaterra Beck past a ruined mine building and a third collapsed adit (**site 6**). Once again there are remnants of a well-constructed tunnel roof. Over the top of the flooded passage is a large chunk of gossan and on top of this you will find another traditional herb – the yellow-flowering St John's wort.

In order to examine the remaining mines, you will need to cross the Glenderaterra Beck (if it's in flood you may wish to avoid this next section by climbing steadily away from the beck until you reach the miners' track that leads back to the car park). Cross at the widest section which can be found further down from the last **adit**. The path continues along the west bank along the top of a broken wall, eventually bringing you to the Glenderaterra Mine (**site 7**).

This mine consists of two vertical shafts from which were driven several horizontal levels. The 'old shaft' as it was called is sited near the ruined minehead buildings and reached a depth of 30 fathoms. A second 'new shaft' was sunk a little further to the south to a depth of 39 fathoms. Both are flooded and in a very dangerous condition.

The huge mounds of spoil between the two shafts contains quartz and the heavier grey crystals of lead sulphide. Notice that there is no grass growing anywhere on this spoil even though it has been left exposed for over 100 years! The only greenery is from a sparse growth of moss that is encroaching along the sides.

After the last pile of spoil, you pass another ruined building. Join the faint miners' track that can be seen running alongside the beck. Where the beck bends sharply to the right, there was a **former bridge**. Cross over (wet feet are unavoidable here unless the river is running low) and follow the now much-clearer track on its way down the valley.

On the right-hand side you pass the **Blencathra Mine** in an area enclosed by a wire fence (opposite a plantation of pines). These lead mines were last worked in the 1870s.

The track now follows a stone wall and then crosses an open area of tall **gorse**. It eventually joins the road leading to Wesco. Almost immediately a path leads off to the left over a stile (sign: 'Footpath'). After crossing several fields, the path brings you back to the Blencathra Centre and your starting point at the car park.

Walk 3

LANTHWAITE WOOD

Only three areas within the Lake District National Park have their own 'Special Sheet' geology maps. They are 'Devoke Water and Ulpha', 'Black Combe' and 'Lorton and Loweswater'. It is significant that Lanthwaite Wood is included on the Lorton map. Here you will find the 'Crummock Water Aureole', with its associated veins of lead and deformed mudstones caused by a massive plug of granite that lies hidden 0.6 mile/1km below the surface.

Recently, Lanthwaite Wood has drawn the attention of botanists who have discovered a new form of green algae growing on its boundary walls. A jelly-like slime has suddenly become a major Lakeland attraction!

But you don't need to wield a geologist's hammer or a botanical hand-lens to enjoy this walk. The lakeside scenery is magnificent: to be enjoyed simply for the moment, or captured on film. And the boat-house is the perfect place for capturing a silhouette at sunset.

THE ROUTE

From the road north of **Lanthwaite Green Farm**, cross the stile and follow the path that leads past the animal pens and farm buildings. The stone wall on your left has a gate (**site 1**). Notice how the base of the wall on each side of this gate is covered in yellow lichen 1.5ft/0.5m up from the ground. Patches of yellow lichen usually indicate high levels of nitrogen from animal waste. The size and position of these yellow patches reflects the territorial habits of the farm's sheepdogs.

Continue along the farm track, crossing a stile and then passing through a gate into **Lanthwaite Wood**. Follow the forest track for about 160ft/50m before turning off left along a narrow path that leads down to the south-east corner of the wood. A small stream runs alongside the path for a short distance before disappearing outside the wood at the end of a boundary wall (**site 2**). Drop down from the path to examine

*The stone steps, handrail and deformed holly trees – a legacy of
Lanthwaite's lead mines (Walk 3)*

the corner of this old wall. The vertical surface facing you is covered in moss on which you will find a bright orange-coloured slime. What you see is a 'green' alga, normally found in tropical rain forests. It is normally green and felt-like: not bright orange and slimy as you see here.

Green algae produce orange and red pigment in well-lit situations. These are the conditions found at this southern edge of the wood where there is less tree cover. But the 'slimy' form is completely unexpected, and so far has not been found anywhere else in Britain. Forget the golden eagles of Mardale – this is Lakeland's latest attraction!

The narrow path now drops steeply away from the wall towards the **boat-house** on the shore of Crummock Water. Once you have reached the shoreline, turn left to make a short detour. After approximately 330ft/100m there is an oak on the right-hand side (**site 3**). Look at the forked trunk and notice how both branches have been split, leaving vertical seams running down their length. It is difficult to be certain what has caused this damage but the length and position of the scars would suggest lightning. An oak is no more likely to be struck by lightning than any other type of tree but perhaps its exposed position down by the lakeside has left it more vulnerable.

Retrace your steps back to the **boat-house** and continue along the forest track. The slope on your right was planted with European larch in the early 50s. It was felled in the mid-80s and has begun to regenerate with native oak and birch. Following this success, the National Trust are felling all the larch on the south side of Boathouse Brow. It is a fact that trees on this warmer south-facing slope grow quicker than on the opposite north-facing side of the valley. From late afternoon onwards, they also receive an extra amount of sunlight reflected off the surface of the lake.

All along this lakeside section where the ground is clear of trees, there are exposed rocks and boulders. You are walking over an area of mudstone that has been baked to a hard, glassy texture. The source of the heat was a huge intrusion of granite which geologists call the 'Crummock Water Aureole'. It lies at a depth of 0.5 mile/1km directly below where you are standing. As you walk north along the side of Crummock Water to **site 4**, you reach the edge of the area of intense heat and the surface mudstones return to their former dull state. (The northern edge of this change-over from metamorphic to sedimentary mudstone follows a line that crosses site 4 and continues running east through Lanthwaite Gate.)

CHECKLIST

Distance: 2.3 miles/3.7km.

Ascent: 260ft/80m.

Approximate Time: 2 hours.

Maps: 1:25 000 OS Outdoor Leisure 4, The English Lakes, North Western area.
1:50 000 OS Landranger 89 or 90.
1:50 000 British Geological Survey, England and Wales Sheet 29, Keswick.
1:25 000 British Geological Survey, Special Sheet NY 12, Lorton and Loweswater (S&D) 1990.

Terrain: The forest tracks are level and well maintained. *The rock steps between sites 5 and 6 are slippery and require care in wet weather.*
If you wish to avoid this difficult section, follow the forest track south to the perimeter gate where the route can be rejoined to reach site 7.

Degree of Shelter: Extremely sheltered inside the woodland.

Stiles: Four.

Special Considerations: Walking this route in the reverse direction is not recommended because of the difficulty in descending the rock steps between sites 5 and 6.

Footwear: Boots.

Parking: Public car park at Lanthwaite Green Farm (NY159208).

Public Transport: Buses from Cockermouth to Buttermere (Stagecoach; service 949, two buses per day on five days a week). Buses from Keswick to Buttermere (Stagecoach; service 77 and 77A, mostly summer).

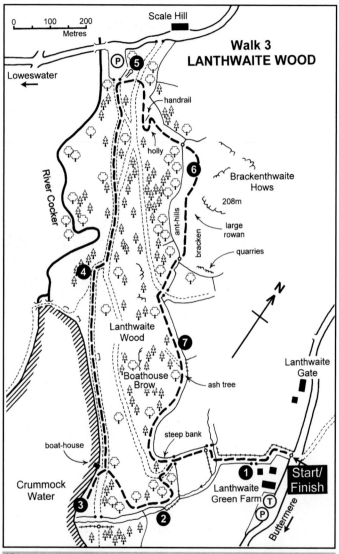

Scale Hill

0   100   200
Metres

Loweswater

**Walk 3
LANTHWAITE WOOD**

handrail

holly

River Cocker

Brackenthwaite
Hows

208m

large
rowan

ant-hills

bracken

quarries

N

Lanthwaite
Wood

Lanthwaite
Gate

Boathouse
Brow

ash tree

boat-house

steep bank

Crummock
Water

Start/
Finish

Lanthwaite
Green Farm

Buttermere

LANTHWAITE WOOD
SITE SUMMARY

1. **Farm gateway (NY158208)**
    Lichen distribution affected by local sheepdogs.

2. **End of boundary wall (NY157206)**
    Growths of a rare jelly-like form of orange-coloured algae.

3. **'Lightning-tree' (NY155205)**
    A forked sessile oak with unusual scars.

4. **Edge of the 'Crummock Water Aureole' (NY152210)**
    North of this point the metamorphic mudstone is replaced by the original sedimentary rock.

5. **Lead Mine (NY149215)**
    Pit and drainage channel associated with local lead mines.

6. **Ant-hill (NY153214)**
    Dark-green grassy mound built by yellow meadow ants.

7. **Old boundary wall (NY155209)**
    Unusual growths of crottle showing spore-producing lobes.

Walk along the forest track until you reach the gate at the National Trust **car park**. As you stand at the gate facing the car park, look at the ground on the right. A broad ditch leads up the slope (partly hidden in undergrowth) and ends in a basin-shaped pit **(site 5)**. There are a

*Bluebells and bracken
outside Lanthwaite Wood –
a sign of deep, fertile soil
and sheltered conditions*

number of adits and trial
tunnels in this area, all of
them seeking out the vein
of lead that crosses the
car park and runs in a
south-easterly direction
across the southern flank
of Brackenthwaite Hows.

The next section of
the route requires care-
ful route-finding. If you
look at the map you will
see a second forest track
entering the wood opposite the
Scale Hill Hotel. You need to
cross over onto this track. The most direct way from the car park gate
is to follow a narrow path that cuts through the short section of woodland just south of site 5. The moment you reach the new track, you
leave it along a narrow miners' path in a south-easterly direction. Study
the map carefully here. The start of this narrow path may be difficult to
find but it is marked on the 1:25 000 OS map at grid reference
NY150215.

Approximately 330ft/100m along this narrow path you reach a
prominent holly tree where the path turns sharp left up a series of steps
cut into the rock. You are now almost level with the vein of lead and
you would expect the vegetation in this area to show signs of metal
poisoning. The holly trees alongside the path do in fact show signs of
disease and distress. Their trunks have cankerous outgrowths and their
leaves are speckled brown.

The path continues to climb steeply up the rock steps alongside a
wooden **handrail** before turning sharp right. Take great care over these
old steps. They are worn smooth and are extremely slippery when wet.

The path now levels off and skirts below the boundary fence and wall. There are lots of bilberry along this section. The trees are mostly sessile oak although there is one struggling Scots pine below the path on the right.

Cross a stile that takes you outside the wood onto the undulating grassland below Brackenthwaite Hows. A narrow, grassy path is followed which drops down to the right alongside some gorse. Look carefully on the right of the path for a dark-green mound of grass (**site 6**). In summer this will be speckled with the tiny white flowers of heath bedstraw. Here is one of many **ant-hills** that have been built on this dry open grassland. It is home of the yellow meadow ant (*Lasius flavus*). The workers range in colour from yellow to golden brown. These raised mounds provide attractive perching-sites for small birds resulting in the grass on top becoming dark-green.

The path keeps to a line about 160ft/50m away from the woodland's boundary wall and passes through an extensive area of **bracken**. Keep a look-out for a large solitary **rowan** on the left and notice how there is no bracken growing below its canopy. This large tree is a favourite shelter for the local sheep and the constant trampling of the ground has kept the bracken in check.

As the path approaches the wall, you pass a birch on the right and then more ant-hills covered in heath bedstraw. The path then loses height with bracken and bluebells on the left. Cross the stile and follow the path steeply down to a gate. Do not go through the gate but turn left following the narrow path that runs inside the boundary wall. After approximately 500ft/150m, take a closer look at the top of this old wall.

You are now at **site 7**. As well as the expected covering of moss, there are fine growths of lichen. The grey-turquoise leaves of crottle are common throughout the district but here it is producing spores from raised lobes on the leaf surface. When the plant produces these structures it indicates that the air is not only moist but also free of pollution.

Continue to follow the wall along to the gate where you first entered the wood and retrace your steps back to the starting point at Lanthwaite Green Farm.

Walk 4

SCALE FORCE

From Victorian times to the present, it would seem that every visitor to Buttermere makes a pilgrimage to Scale Force. The aim is to see the waterfall, and the route to it becomes just a means to that end. When guidebooks do mention the paths they only recall how muddy they are!

The walk described here will not escape the mud but it will show that there is more to this popular outing than just getting there and back. In fact the path takes us past two lakes and two separate waterfalls. It crosses two major areas of geology, with a detour to a hidden valley. The ground is wet but all this makes for some interesting plantlife.

At 120ft/37m, Scale Force is the longest uninterrupted plunge of water in Cumbria. The height is such that the upward currents of displaced air break up the water droplets to form a constant suspension. This results in humidity levels of 100 per cent within the narrow confines of the gorge which supports a very localised community of mosses and ferns. The 120ft drop also results in the water temperature at the base of the fall being marginally higher than at the top as the potential and kinetic energy is converted into heat.

You can of course stand below the fall without the physics and just enjoy the grandure. After all, this is the home of the Romantics.

THE ROUTE

Start at the Fish Hotel, **Buttermere**, and follow the famously muddy path that leads to Scale Bridge. The first thing you notice are the red stones that make up the path surface. You are now entering an area of red granite and the names on the map reflect this.

The long straight lane with a hedge of blackthorn and willow leads

CHECKLIST

Distance:	4.1 miles/6.6km.
Ascent:	650ft/200m.
Approximate Time:	4 hours.
Maps:	1:25 000 OS Leisure 4, The English Lakes, North Western area. 1:50 000 OS Landranger 89. 1:50 000 British Geological Survey, England and Wales Sheet 29, Keswick.
Terrain:	The lower paths are wet and indistinct in places. The return path from Scale Force is rough and deeply eroded.
Degree of Shelter:	The route is sheltered from strong westerly winds. The large oak trees alongside Far Ruddy Beck provides the only shelter from heavy rain.
Stiles:	None.
Special Considerations:	None.
Footwear:	Waterproof boots.
Parking:	Public car park next to the Fish Hotel (NY174169).
Public Transport:	Summer bus service from Keswick passing through Buttermere (Stagecoach; service 77 and 77A).

you to the smooth-flowing river that connects Buttermere with Crummock Water. The path bends right towards Scale Bridge (**site 1**). As you approach the bridge take a close look at the plants on the left of the path. As well as the familiar yellow iris growing on the water's edge, look for **apple mint** alongside a line of large stones. The bridge itself has fine growths of maidenhair spleenwort fern growing on the lime mortar.

After crossing the bridge, turn right. For the next few hundred metres the path becomes even wetter as it crosses three separate streams. Along this section you will find large specimens of carnivo-

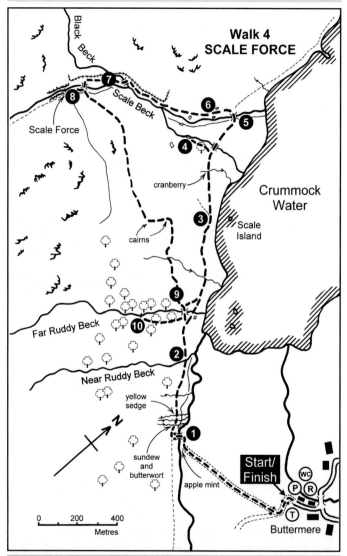

Black Beck

Scale Beck

Walk 4
SCALE FORCE

Scale Force

cranberry

Crummock
Water

cairns

Scale Island

Far Ruddy Beck

Near Ruddy Beck

yellow sedge

N

sundew and butterwort

apple mint

Start/
Finish

WC

P   R

T

Buttermere

0   200   400
Metres

SCALE FORCE
SITE SUMMARY

1. **Scale Bridge (NY168166)**
   Apple mint growing alongside large stones on approach path.

2. **Near Ruddy Beck (NY165168)**
   Birch tree resting on rock covered in crottle.

3. **Path junction (NY159174)**
   Distinct change from marshy grassland to bracken where underlying mudstone replaces peat.

4. **Hidden valley (NY156175)**
   Grove of decaying birch trees covered in razor-strop fungus.

5. **Broken wall (NY157178)**
   Round stones with distinct circular lichen colonies reflecting the lack of cleavage-plains within granite.

6. **Stony mound on path (NY155176)**
   Site of ant-hill and territorial marking-area for local foxes.

7. **Scale Beck (NY151173)**
   Boulder-strewn water-course with dried-up overflow channels.

8. **Scale Force (NY151171)**
   Vein of haematite with evidence of previous mining activity.

9. **Change in path colour (NY162170)**
   Boundary of sedimentary grey mudstone and red granite.

10. **Hidden waterfall (NY162168)**
    Spectacular falls in wooded ravine. Rarely visited.

rous plants. The **sundew** grows here; its deadly leaves arranged like a rosette of red table-tennis bats. They are covered in long sticky tentacles that move very slowly to engulf any small insect that happens to land on them. You can get the same response by dropping a small piece of cheese onto one of the leaves. They are hungry for nitrogen found in the protein. The **butterwort** looks like a pale green starfish and the in-rolled leaves are flooded with sticky fluid that digests any unsuspecting midge in a matter of hours.

In early summer keep a look-out for the heath-spotted orchid along this left bank and as you cross the third stream look down amongst the grass for **yellow sedge**, the tops of which resemble tiny yellow pineapples.

After crossing another small stream, you pass a large holly on your right before reaching **Near Ruddy Beck** at **site 2**. Notice the birch tree with the base of its trunk bent over a rock. The west-facing side of this rock is covered in lichen. Of the 1400 or so species of lichen found in Britain, there are only about 20 that have been given common English names – and this is one of them. It is called 'crottle' and was used for dying wool in the Scottish islands. The colour produced was golden brown and the dyed cloth had a very distinct smell. If you own some old Harris Tweed you'll notice this as soon as it gets wet.

Before reaching Far Ruddy Beck, the path forks (marked by a cairn). The original route followed the right-hand branch and crossed the beck over stepping-stones, but since the building of the wooden footbridge, almost everyone now takes the higher left-hand branch. If the water-level is high, cross the beck using the footbridge but then immediately drop down to rejoin the lower path. Suddenly, it's as though you've gone back 100 years – when this was the main tourist route to Scale Force. If you do meet anyone, you half expect to see Norfolk jackets and long dresses! Today's visitors have been drawn by the bridge into following the higher path, leaving the lower path almost deserted.

The price for solitude is wet feet. This lower path gets even wetter and because it is out of favour, it is indistinct in places. Try keeping the same height above Crummock Water. When you are opposite **Scale Island** you may notice an indistinct fork in the path climbing gently up to the left through an area of bracken (**site 3**). Don't take this route but keep straight on, aiming for the trees in front. Even though the path seems to disappear in the boggy ground (look out for **cranberries** in this section), keep faith and you will reach a wooden footbridge that crosses Scale Beck. Now it feels that you really have gone back in time. Half a mile away is one of the busiest paths in the Lake District and here is a route that takes you over a bridge that is almost completely forgotten.

Before crossing, it is worth making a short detour to the left following the course of the beck through the trees for a few hundred metres. The water-course divides and joins up again in a sheltered grove of dead and decaying trees (**site 4**). This section of the beck is set down and completely hidden from above. Look closely at the birch trees. They are covered in a bracket fungus – the 'razor-strop fungus'. Its leathery surface was once used to sharpen razors. It only grows on birch and it invariably kills the tree.

Retrace your steps back to the footbridge. Once over the other side you step onto drier ground onto what is in fact an island delta between the split water-course of Scale Beck. The drier ground favours colonies of the yellow meadow ant. Their characteristic nests are found in raised grassy mounds (one prominent nest is to the right of the path, just 80ft/25m before the next footbridge).

Before crossing this bridge take a look at the broken-down wall running along the side of the beck (**site 5**). It's a good place to practise your lichen-spotting and to see if you can find some more crottle. Most of the colonies on these rocks are perfectly circular which indicates that the granite structure has no side-to-side 'grain' for plantlife to follow. This also explains why granite walls are more difficult to construct since most of the stones are rounded and show little tendency to split into thin slabs.

After crossing the bridge, follow the path left passing some ruined sheepfolds. At this point the path goes over a stony mound on top of which is an ant-hill (**site 6**). This slightly elevated feature has great significance for the local fox population. It is a territorial marking-post and a careful examination of the ant-hill should reveal fox-droppings.

The narrow stony path now rises gently between patches of gorse and after passing a solitary hawthorn it runs alongside a wire fence. There are some unusual contrasts in the wild flowers along this section. Look down at the rocks on the edge of the path and you will see wild thyme whilst just to the right at the base of the fence there is sundew growing on cushions of sphagnum.

The path passes the junction of **Scale Beck** with its tributary, **Black Beck**, which is crossed by a footbridge. You are now on a steep tongue

On the return path to Scale Bridge, with Honister Crag on the skyline

of land between the two becks (**site 7**). A few hundred metres in front, you get your first view of Scale Force pouring into its tree-lined gorge. Scale Beck on your left has had its course altered many times by the force of water. If you look down below the path you will see the course it once followed – now quite dry.

At the top of this stony spur you pass between two iron posts which is all that survives of the old Victorian 'gateway'. Drop down to cross the wooden footbridge and then scramble as far as you can up the left side of the beck for a close-up view of **Scale Force**, Lakeland's longest waterfall (**site 8**). At the base of the fall, try finding evidence of past mining activity – one of five exploratory levels that were dug into a band of iron deposits that runs from Floutern Tarn to Crummock Water.

Return to the footbridge and go through the gap in the wall to join the 'higher' path that leads back to Buttermere. The red gravelly soil around the wall is coming from the vein of iron that runs up the left side of the gorge. The path you are about to follow is also tinged red due to the colour of the local granite. Unlike the lower path, it is deeply eroded.

As you approach Far Ruddy Beck, the colour of the path suddenly changes to a dull grey (**site 9**). This marks the position of an exposed area of Skiddaw 'slate' along the granite boundary.

Continue down to the wooden footbridge over **Far Ruddy Beck**. If it's raining heavily you can shelter here amongst the large oaks that grow on each side of the beck. This is the setting for another waterfall, but this one cannot be seen from the path and requires a 15 minute detour.

After crossing the bridge, walk on for about 50ft/15m and then turn off to the right, through the trees (well away from the edge of the ravine). There is no single path here even though Wainwright shows one for the ascent of Red Pike (see *The Western Fells*; Red Pike, 6). The way up through the trees is quite steep but is well worth the effort. Across to your right you can hear the waterfall (**site 10**). It has no name and is hardly ever visited. Those who have seen it will inevitably compare it with Scale Force. Comparison is unfair, except to say that when some visitors to Buttermere were asked if they'd seen 'the waterfall', they replied 'which one?'

Retrace your steps via sites 2 and 1 back to the car park.

Walk 5

JOHNNY WOOD AND SCALECLOSE COPPICE

Welcome to Borrowdale – the wettest place in England! As you travel up the valley and through its 'jaws', the annual rainfall rises dramatically from 178cm at Keswick to 318cm at Seathwaite. What are we doing here, you may ask? Do we really want to walk into this? Couldn't we just sit it out in a cafe or pub or something? Well, all is not lost. This valley contains the largest area of native woodland in the Lake District and that means there is shelter beneath the trees.

Six Borrowdale woods have been identified as Sites of Special Scientific Interest (SSSIs): Castle Head Wood, The Ings, Great Wood, Lodore and Troutdale Woods, Johnny Wood, and Seatoller Wood. As a group they are of international importance for their variety of ferns, mosses, liverworts and lichens for which they have been given the status of a Grade 1 site. In Seathwaite Wood alone, 111 species of lichen have been recorded – so tread softly for you tread on a botanist's dreams!

For this walk you will be entering Johnny Wood and its outlier, Scaleclose Coppice. Both contain sessile oak that has been coppiced for making charcoal. But since this industry finished over 100 years ago, the woods have now been left to nature.

There is an element of entering a lost world. Whilst everyone is rushing up and down the valley or clambering over the summit ridges, these woods offer a quiet refuge and shelter. The loudest noise you are likely to hear is a woodpecker looking for grubs.

THE ROUTE

The walk begins at **Longthwaite Youth Hostel**. Take the gravel path heading south past the Warden's house through a gate to **site 1**. On

CHECKLIST

Distance:	3.3 miles/5.4km.
Ascent:	850ft/260m.
Approximate Time:	3 hours.
Maps:	1:25 000 OS Outdoor Leisure 4, The English Lakes, North Western area. 1:50 000 OS Landranger 90.
Terrain:	Gentle woodland paths with some short steep sections.
Degree of Shelter:	Very sheltered in the woodland sections. Exposed on the fellside below High Doat (283m).
Stiles:	Three (one optional, alongside gate).
Special Considerations:	The woodlands are internationally important SSSIs. Please keep to the paths. Take particular care when crossing Scaleclose Gill by the new footbridge to avoid the loose gravel that forms the gill sides. Please do not pick or disturb any of the plants. They grow here because of the especially wet conditions. A removed plant will quickly become a dead specimen. If you want a record, take a photo.
Footwear:	Boots.
Parking:	Public car park and toilets at Rosthwaite (NY257148). Please note that parking at Longthwaite Youth Hostel is for patrons only.
Public Transport:	Buses from Keswick to Rosthwaite and Seatoller (Stagecoach; service 79 every hour).

the opposite side of the river notice the high bank of loose gravelly soil with occasional large boulders. This is a glacial moraine left by the snout of a retreating glacier that once filled the Stonethwaite Valley. It is the first of three terminal moraines which can be seen as three

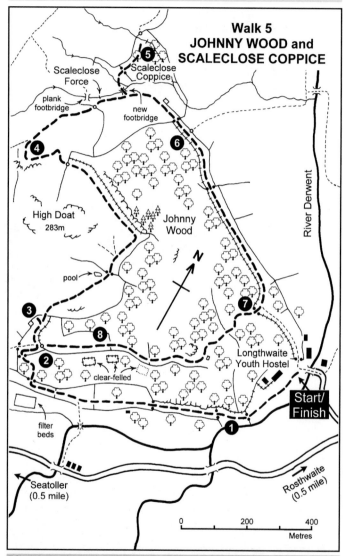

Walk 5
**JOHNNY WOOD and
SCALECLOSE COPPICE**

Scaleclose
Force

Scaleclose
Coppice

5

plank
footbridge

new
footbridge

4

6

High Doat
283m

Johnny
Wood

N

pool

River Derwent

3

7

8

Longthwaite
Youth Hostel

2

clear-felled

1

Start/
Finish

filter
beds

Seatoller
(0.5 mile)

Rosthwaite
(0.5 mile)

0   200   400
                  Metres

JOHNNY WOOD AND SCALECLOSE COPPICE
SITE SUMMARY

1. **Bend in river (NY254141)**
    Evidence of former riverbed diverted by glacial moraine.

2. **'Pitstead' (NY248140)**
    Level circular clearing where the coppiced oak was burnt for making charcoal.

3. **Yew tree (NY247141)**
    500 year old specimen alongside traditional Lakeland barn.

4. **A puzzling boulder (NY245145)**
    Why does this particular boulder have a yellow top?

5. **Hidden waterfall (NY247149)**
    Atmospheric ravine alongside iron seepage and strange growths of moss.

6. **Tree-lined path (NY249148)**
    Signs of feeding roe deer.

7. **Path junction (NY253144)**
    Quiet path leads into heart of Johnny Wood. Alternative route heads directly back to Longthwaite Youth Hostel.

8. **Bracken-filled clearing (NY250141)**
    Sessile oaks with aerial polypody. Three experimental plots showing forest regeneration.

The 'puzzling boulder' at site 4 with Castle Crag in the background

concentric mounds curving through the village of Rosthwaite. Each time the ice retreated it left a deposit of what it was carrying – similar to the lines of seaweed stranded on a beach.

The moraine that you can see on the opposite bank diverted the river coming down the Seathwaite Valley and changed the course of the Derwent at this point by squeezing it westwards. The ice and rubble held the riverbed much higher than its present level and forced the water to flow against the hard volcanic rock on the west bank. If you look at the smooth polished rock alongside the path (next to the chains that have been conveniently strung across for handholds), you will see the former riverbed. It is at least 16ft/5m higher than the present level. The constant force of water carrying small stones has left smoothed-out basins and channels in the rock.

Follow the path through two more gates following the well-built stone wall on your left until you reach the sewage **filter beds**. Turn off right through a small gate, taking the steep path that leads into Johnny Wood. This is a long-established wood of sessile oaks (sessile means that the acorns are without stalks). These trees were coppiced regularly every 10 to 15 years for making charcoal.

The path leads up through another gate where you follow the farm track right, passing two white stones. These stones were most likely selected and placed on the sharp bends to help navigate farm vehicles at night. The stones have been cleaned of lichen and moss and show the colour of the Borrowdale Volcanic rock found at this point. The rock is white because of its high silica content and because of the bleaching effect of the peaty water from where they were taken.

Where the path reaches the second white stone, look down over the wall to **site 2**. Here, 33ft/10m down from the wall, you will see a flat circular clearing built up level on a platform of stones. This is a 'pitstead', one of the best-preserved examples in the area. It was here that the coppiced oak was stacked wigwam-style and left to smoulder slowly under a covering of turf to make charcoal.

Continue following the path alongside the wire fence then take a short detour left towards a large yew tree (**site 3**). Yews live a long time. This one is probably over 500 years old – a young tree compared with the 2000 year old Seathwaite Yew made famous as one of Wordsworth's 'Fraternal Four'.

The roofless building in front is an old barn where animals were kept. The oak beams that supported the hayloft are still on site. What clues are there that animals were kept here? Look around the ruined walls for nettles: a sure sign of high nitrogen levels left from animal manure. And on the ground that was once disturbed by animal hooves, foxgloves grow amongst the scattered stones.

Continue on the path upwards through a gap in the wall. The path is less distinct at this point but head straight up the grassy slope and aim for a prominent holly tree on the skyline. Pass through the gap between the holly and an ash after which the ground dips down to a small **pool**. Go straight on through the gate following the path that leads to a large cairn built unusually in a sunken hollow.

Here the path splits. The left-hand branch leads up to the summit of High Doat: a fine viewpoint on a clear day. Our misty route is along to the right, following the wall which forms the west boundary of **Johnny Wood**. A steep narrow path bears left alongside a barbed-wire fence.

This is the highest and most exposed part of the walk. Follow the fence until you reach a wall. Cross by the stile near a hawthorn and descend the grassy slope to **site 4**. Here is a puzzle to take your mind off the driving rain. Where the slope levels out there is a large solitary boulder. Look at the lichen growing on it and notice the different types growing in different places. On the north side there are cup lichens, sheltering from the prevailing wind. The top of this boulder (like so many other isolated boulders seen on these walks) is covered in a crust of mustard-coloured lichen called *Candelariella*. The Latin name may be off-putting but the question remains – why does this lichen grow on the top and not down the sides of such a large isolated rock? The clues should be here. Look carefully at the top… and the bird-droppings. This prominent boulder in this open area is a favourite lookout-perch for the local birdlife and over time the droppings have affected the surface-chemistry of the rock. *Candelariella* grows here because of the nitrogen.

To the south is a large birch growing in wet ground below a wall of crags. Take a close look at its branches and examine where they join the central trunk. Here you will find a bilberry plant growing about 6.5ft/2m off the ground. On the crags above are more birch one of which looks as if it is full of crows' nests. These are 'witches' brooms' – where a fungus has infected the buds causing the extra growth to appear like nests.

Take the indistinct grassy path north which leads past two isolated

Polypody on branch of sessile oak

fenceposts before reaching a steep ladder-stile. Once over the stile, the path turns right down a pleasant grassy embankment with Scaleclose Gill on your left. About 65ft/20m down from the stile, **Scaleclose Force** can be seen by carefully peering down between the birch and ash trees that line the sides of the ravine.

Continue down the grassy path for a short distance and turn left at the National Trust sign to Scaleclose Coppice. Descend the narrow gravelly path into the gill and carefully cross the stream using the **new footbridge**.

Continue on the path out of the ravine until you reach the gate into the **Scaleclose Coppice**. The narrow path climbs gently through the oak wood, keeping a few metres below the west boundary wall until reaching the top where a stream enters. You are now at **site 5**. There is something special about this place. Before crossing the stream, walk carefully 16ft/5m off to the right and look down into the ravine that forms the north-east boundary of this woodland. Here is a waterfall with no name and one that rivals any in Lakeland for atmosphere. Its wispy trail drops 160ft/50m into a narrow gorge filled with hart's-tongue fern, woodrush and wild garlic. This is uncharted territory in the heart of Lakeland. The last time I stood here, a red squirrel sat on the holly tree that juts out over the drop behind you. A roe deer has gnawed the same tree.

Now head back to the path where the stream enters the coppice. Look at the bright orange seepage coming out from under the wall above the stream (by a dead ash with honeysuckle growing over it). This is iron coming out of the wet boggy region just outside the coppice. If conditions are right, you can detect the smell of bad eggs in this mineral soup!

Before retracing your steps, take a final look at the oak trees and notice the straggly growths of moss on their bark. It is all drawn out to one side. The trailing filaments are all slanting down, as if they have been pulled towards the waterfall in the ravine. This is a strange place! As you stand here, you will be sheltered from all but the westerly winds which are drawn down into the narrow ravine like a funnel. It is the only strong wind these mosses experience – a downdraft into the water-fall towards which they grow as if drawn by a magnet.

Retrace your steps back to the National Trust sign to rejoin the gently-sloping path heading back to Longthwaite. Pass through a gate leading to a tree-lined path (**site 6**). There have been many examples on this walk of how birds can affect where plants grow: lichens on rocks, bilberries in trees. Here we have trees within trees. Look for a mature holly on your left growing out of the forked branches of an oak (alongside a honeysuckle). Notice also how many trees bordering the path along this section have their roots gnawed. You are still inside the territory of a male roe deer.

Continue on through another gate along the tree-lined path until you reach a small gate in the wire fence on your right at **site 7**. (If you wish to shorten the walk at this point, continue straight ahead following the main path which leads back to the Youth Hostel.) To continue into the heart of this quiet woodland, turn right through the gate. The narrow path leads into a level clearing before climbing steeply, snaking its way through exposed tree roots and leaf-litter. When you reach the wall at the top, go through the gap (marked with a yellow arrow on its south side) and follow the forest path. You pass a small ruined building after which the path swings right at a second yellow waymark. Many of the large oaks along this next section have green plastic identification tabs, each tree being recorded by the National Trust with its own number.

Notice that every time the path becomes boggy, there is almost always a holly tree just alongside – indicating how the slightest change in soil moisture affects tree distribution. When passing these hollies, there may be one with fresh bird-lime underneath. Move slowly and check the upper branches for a resident tawny owl, a bird that often chooses holly for its daytime roosting site.

Eventually the path leads into a bracken-filled clearing at **site 8**. On the south side of the wall that you have been following there are three rectangular areas that have been **clear-felled** as an experiment in forest regeneration. The first site is unfenced; the second is fenced to keep out sheep and the third is fenced against deer. Look at the large oaks next to these newly fenced enclosures. Many have ferns growing high up on their branches. This is the polypody fern, some of which is found here growing 33ft/10m above the ground.

The path continues through bracken, past a single young birch, until you reach the stile that takes you outside the wood. From here, retrace your route back to Rosthwaite via Longthwaite Youth Hostel or continue on down to Seatoller.

Walk 6

WATENDLATH

Some parts of Lakeland are visited because of the distant views and when the mist and rain comes down there is very little to hold the eye. Watendlath is different. Even when visibility is down to 160ft/50m, there is enough here to enjoy.

The valley has been carefully managed by the National Trust who maintain those delicate countryside features that now characterise the English Lake District. Here you can expect to see stone walls, pollarded trees and a traditional working hill farm. But as this walk shows, there is much to find that is unexpected and often overlooked.

Part of Watendlath's charm depends upon the special combination of volcanic rocks, extensive peat deposits and a high rainfall. You may find equally wet ground in other parts of Lakeland but you rarely find such a variety of associated wetland plants. There may be larger waterfalls elsewhere but nothing can match the setting of 'The Devil's Punchbowl'.

This is a place that continues to attract artists and photographers seeking to find the 'traditional Lakeland view'. But there is more to Watendlath than its famous calendar image. Here is a walk especially for that rainy day when the crowds have left and the tops are out of bounds. Here is a chance to enjoy Watendlath at close quarters.

THE ROUTE

Starting from the National Trust **car park**, make your way past Fold Head Farm to the packhorse bridge (**site 1**). Along with Ashness Bridge further down the valley, this is one of the most photographed sites in Lakeland. Its cobbled surface was relaid in 1995 during the National Trust's centenary year. A temporary wooden bridge was constructed alongside whilst work was underway. Look carefully on the grass bank to the left of the old bridge and you will find the sawn-off foundation

CHECKLIST

Distance:	2.3 miles/3.7km.
Ascent:	300ft/90m.
Approximate Time:	2 hours.
Maps:	1:25 000 OS Outdoor Leisure 4, The English Lakes, North Western area. 1:50 000 OS Landranger 90. 1:50 000 British Geological Survey, England and Wales Sheet 29, Keswick.
Terrain:	Clearly marked footpaths, mostly dry except between sites 5 and 6.
Degree of Shelter:	A low-level walk that is well sheltered except for the moorland crossing between sites 5 and 8.
Stiles:	Two (one of which is optional alongside gate).
Special Considerations:	The road to Watendlath from Ashness is narrow single-track with passing places and can be extremely busy mid-morning and late afternoon – a good reason for leaving the car and taking the National Trust shuttle-bus.
Footwear:	Boots.
Parking:	National Trust car park (NY276163).
Public Transport:	The National Trust operate a free Sunday bus service between Keswick and Watendlath (telephone the National Trust Regional Office, 015394 35599, for details).

poles (two on each side). If you look carefully behind these wooden stumps on the far side, you can see two metal tubes set into the ground where the tensioning cables had been attached.

Prince Charles was invited to lay a commemorative stone in the cobble surface. It is difficult to find amongst all the other stones but

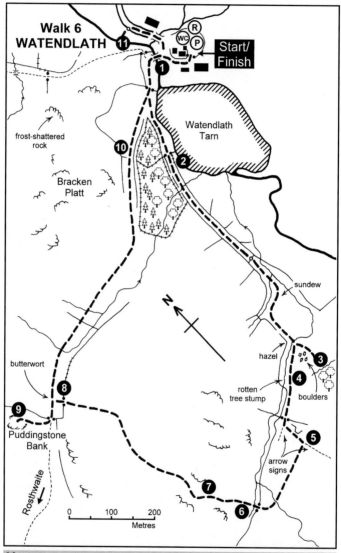

Walk 6
WATENDLATH

Start/Finish

Watendlath Tarn

frost-shattered rock

Bracken Platt

sundew

hazel

butterwort

rotten tree stump

boulders

arrow signs

Puddingstone Bank

Rosthwaite

0   100   200
Metres

N

Watendlath, an aerial view from the path to High Tove (Walk 6)

The extraordinary walls of Grassguards (Walk 10)

Primary and secondary rainbows at Aira Force (Walk 11) (© Heather Lyon)

WATENDLATH – SITE SUMMARY

1. **Packhorse bridge (NY275163)**
   Commemorative stone laid by Prince Charles. Group of polypody fern growing down from underside of arch.

2. **Wire fence (NY274162)**
   The complex ecology of a Lakeland fencepost.

3. **Natural birch wood (NY274155)**
   An unusual group of ash, hazel and birch with a parasitic juniper.

4. **Stone mosaic (NY273156)**
   Badge-like pattern built alongside reconstructed path.

5. **Path junction (NY272154)**
   Right-hand fork with sign to Puddingstone Bank. Water-logged peat with large area of scented bog myrtle.

6. **Isolated boulder (NY270154)**
   Bird-pellets and rock tripe indicate kestrel feeding perch.

7. **Roche moutonnée (NY269155)**
   Cylinder-shaped rock polished smooth by ice.

8. **Wooden bench (NY268159)**
   Rushes, lesser spearwort, sundew and bog bean in water-logged peat.

9. **Puddingstone Bank (NY267159)**
   Views of upper Borrowdale and Johnny Wood.

10. **Viewpoint ((NY273162)**
    View north to frost-shattered rock face.

11. **'The Churn' (NY275165)**
    Series of cascades flowing through smoothed-out rock basins.

The view of upper Borrowdale from Puddingstone Bank –
Johnny Wood can be seen left of centre

look for one on this far side with the inscription: HRH CHARLES
22–5–95.

Hanging from the underside of the arch is a group of ferns normally
found growing on trees. This is polypody thriving in the moist sheltered
conditions out of reach of the grazing sheep.

From the bridge, follow the footpath that leads left alongside
Watendlath Tarn. Pass through the gate and follow the path, keeping
left at the signpost to Dock Tarn. As you cross a small stream, look for
spearmint at the water's edge. Another gate takes you alongside a
freshly pollarded ash with a wire fence on your left that leads to a
sycamore. You are now at **site 2**. Look at the wooden post at the end of
this section of wire fence below the sycamore. This sheltered path
bordered by a combination of fence and stone wall is a lichen-hunter's
delight. Here on this square corner post, the lichens have begun to
colonise the wood surface, but like most wooden posts along here it is
only the top that is covered. Lichen is transported on the feet of birds

and growth is encouraged by bird-droppings. What is most striking is that these plants tend not to spread below the line of the top wire and staple. The effect is seen to its best after heavy rain. The iron-stains on the wood are quite bare, showing the poisonous effect of rust on lichen growth.

Continue along the path with its ancient line of pollarded ash. The wire fence now gives way to stone walls on which can be found specimens of cup lichen and a rather unusual moss (*Rhacomitrium lanuginosum*) normally found on high mountain tundra. The moss looks like it is covered in frizzy strands of wool which turn a characteristic greeny-grey when dry. This has given it the popular name: 'wooly' or 'frizzy-hair moss'.

After crossing a stile, the path climbs gently along the right-hand side of a stream. Cross the stream into an open grassy area which leads across a boggy section with **sundew** on each side of the path. A little further along you cross another stream with a **hazel** growing at the bend in the wall. Notice how the thick patches of moss appear to be dripping off its horizontal branches.

The main path is indicated by an arrow-sign pointing up to the right. At this point take a short detour following the left-hand fork. You are now on a level grassy track that once led into the oak wood that covered much of the slopes on this side of the valley. The oaks were felled for timber and the soils became more acid on exposure to the high rainfall. The woodland, known as West Side Wood, regenerated itself as a birch wood.

After skirting around an open area with scattered **boulders**, the path goes between two hazels before reaching the first birch. It is part of a curious group of three trees on the left side of the path (**site 3**). Hazel, ash and birch grow alongside each other as if out of the same base. The central ash has been coppiced. Look carefully at this ash with its fine growth of polypody. At first glance it looks as if someone has attached a hanging-basket high up in its branches. To the left of the sawn-off crown, a juniper has taken root, its seed having been deposited some years ago by a bird. Juniper trees often have different forms, sometimes growing upright and sometimes sideways. Here it is growing downwards.

Retrace your steps (about 500ft/150m) back to the path junction and follow the arrow taking you up the left side of the stream. Look for an ash next to a **rotten tree stump** on your right. The path in front of you is about to get steeper and has been carefully reconstructed with stones where it was becoming badly eroded. Look carefully to the left of the path (**site 4**). Amongst the grass and measuring about 6.5ft/2m across is a symmetrical mosaic pattern made out of tightly packed stones (built perhaps by one of the volunteer path workers).

The path climbs and then crosses a very boggy section before passing through a gate in a stone wall. You now meet the first of many **arrow signs** requesting walkers to avoid the former path to prevent damaging the wetland area. The path you are now following leads to a set of large stepping-stones. Do not follow the stepping-stones (they lead to Dock Tarn). Instead, take the right-hand fork at another sign (**site 5**), following the arrow 'to Puddingstone Bank and Rosthwaite'.

This wetland area has one of the finest stands of bog myrtle in the Lake District. It is a plant that says much about the underlying geology. Its distinctive scent becomes associated with certain areas (walk from Wasdale to Eskdale over Irton Fell and you can smell the change as you cross from Borrowdale Volcanic into Eskdale Granite!). Here, at Watendlath, we have crossed from fertile volcanic rock onto an area of acid gravel overlaid with peat.

The other characteristic plant of this type of wetland is bog asphodel. In late summer look for its clusters of yellow star-shaped flowers. In winter look for the dead straw-like stalks of last year's growth.

The path now follows a line of posts with green-painted tops. After crossing a stream, keep a look-out for star sedge, so named because of the star-shaped clusters of seeds held on the ends of its thin stems. Also along this section, you may have noticed another feature of poorly drained peat bogs – a thin film of 'oil' covering the surface water.

Pass through the gate in the stone wall and after approximately 100ft/30m you will find a low outcrop of rock to the left of the path (**site 6**). This particular outcrop has been used by various birds as a perch (after being deprived of a dry landmark over much of this feature-less wetland). The effect on the rock surface will now be familiar but is always satisfying to find – patches of mustard-coloured *Candelariella* on the highest points, with rock tripe scattered in-between. The food-pellets are the right size to be from a kestrel.

Continue over a boggy section across stepping-stones until you come alongside a steep crag on your left. To the right of the path (**site 7**) is a smooth length of rock that has been shaped and polished by ice. Because of their frequent resemblance to resting sheep, such rocks are known as *roches moutonnées*, only this one looks more like a stone submarine!

After crossing more stepping-stones, the path passes between two isolated hawthorns before leading through a gate. You are now at **site 8**. To the right of the path is a simple wooden bench. Notice the rushes growing underneath it. In poor rural areas, the central pith of this particular plant (soft rush) was removed and dipped in animal fat to make rush lamps as an alternative to candles.

Opposite the bench is another familiar wetland plant – the lesser spearwort – which can be distinguished from the meadow buttercup by its long spear-shaped leaves. In a boggy area like this you will almost always find sundew, but this particular area is so poorly drained, there are also water-plants normally only found submerged in mountain tarns. About 20ft/6m past the bench and to the left of the path is a patch of bog bean, its leaves poking through the surface water in groups of three. If you are here in May or June, you will see it in full flower – the most delicate clusters of white lace-like petals fringed with flecks of pink.

'The Churn' or 'Devil's Punchbowl' at site 11

Above Watendlath Tarn on the approach to site 2

This area also shows the characteristic oily film often found on peat moorland. This coloured film is not oil but a thin layer of either insoluble iron oxide or bacteria. The colour patterns (Newton's rings) depend on a parallel film stretching across the surface of the water. The thinner the layer of iron or bacteria, the more intense the colour that is produced.

The path now joins the main walking route from Rosthwaite to Watendlath. If the weather is clear, it is worthwhile making a short detour to climb **Puddingstone Bank** (**site 9**). This provides splendid views across into upper Borrowdale with Johnny Wood and the Langstrath Valley in the distance.

Rejoin the broad gravelly path leading down into Watendlath (excellent specimens of **butterwort** and sundew on the left-hand side). The resurfaced path eventually gets steeper as you pass plantations of larch on the right. The path is joined by stone walls on each side. After passing through a gap (**site 10**), there is a view to the left of a spectacular **frost-shattered rock**, split like a cascade of falling dominoes. The rock on this side of the valley is andesite larva some of which is extremely brittle and contains small garnets.

The path leads down to the packhorse bridge. Cross the bridge and then turn left to join the valley road. Cross the road bridge over Raise Gill and look for a stile in the roadside wall up ahead on your left (the road at this point swings right).

Follow the little-used narrow path leading down from the stile to Watendlath Beck (**site 11**). Here is a surprise feature that is often over-looked. It is a waterfall variously known as 'The Churn' or 'The Devil's Punchbowl' and in Victorian times was one of the main attractions in the area. What makes this cascade unusual are the hidden drainage channels cut into the volcanic rock. The water going into the top basin or 'churn' doesn't all come out over the rim! Instead, it escapes through various unseen cracks to reappear under pressure in the foaming pool below.

From here, retrace your steps back to the stile, returning along the road to your starting point at the car park.

Walk 7

HIGH-LEVEL ROUTE (PILLAR)

Certain mountain walks become classics. The High-Level Route on Pillar is one. You can tell by the name that this isn't going to be a casual Sunday afternoon outing.

Pillar Fell takes its name from the adjoining Pillar Rock. The High-Level Route connects them both. Most people climbing Pillar Fell will simply follow the skyline from the top of Black Sail Pass unaware of Pillar Rock except for a suggestion of a craggy buttress hidden somewhere below.

On this route, the Rock dominates the view. There is an element of danger and you will need to concentrate, especially when it's wet and misty. You need to be able to use a map and compass and you need boots and good mountain clothing. It is safer with a companion rather than alone.

The route described here is presented as a walk in its own right, but it can be fitted into a visit to the summit ridge or used to add an interesting diversion to the route over Black Sail Pass. It can be tackled from either direction and if staying at the Ennerdale Youth Hostels, it makes an ideal expedition connecting the two.

The orientation of the Pillar ridge is parallel with the prevailing westerly winds. There is no break or 'wind gap' along the section from Pillar Rock to Looking Stead and the spurs and coves serve to produce complex eddy currents and down-drafts held at a distance from the path. This means that during a spell of wet and misty weather, walkers on the High-Level Route can witness dramatic air movements made visible by the moving cloud vapours.

For the same reason, the summit ridge is one of the best places in the district for seeing the 'brocken spectre' when the sun casts your shadow onto mist in the coves below.

Many would say the High-Level Route is not a place for a

CHECKLIST

Distance:	5 miles/8km. Connecting Ennerdale and Black Sail youth hostels. The High-Level Route from Pillar Rock to Looking Stead is only 1 mile/1.5km in length.
Ascent:	1800ft/550m.
Approximate Time:	If wet, allow 3 to 5 hours from hostel to hostel.
Maps:	1:25 000 OS Leisure 4, The English Lakes, North Western area. 1:50 000 OS Landranger 89. 1:50 000 British Geological Survey, England and Wales Sheet 29, Keswick.
Terrain:	Forest roads in the Ennerdale Valley. Steep and slippery sections along the forest ride and fellside below Pillar Rock. The High-Level Route itself is undulating with rocky sections requiring concentration and some scrambling in places.
Degree of Shelter:	Sheltered in the forest sections. Once above the tree-line, the route is open to the north and east but is surprisingly sheltered from the prevailing south-westerly winds.
Stiles:	One.
Special Considerations:	This is a remote area and in misty conditions in particular it is important to inform others of your intended route and destination. *In wet weather, this route is for the experienced hillwalker only.*
Footwear:	Boots with good grip.
Parking:	Bowness Knott public car park, Ennerdale Water (NY109154), situated 2 miles/3km from the youth hostel at Gillerthwaite (parking at hostel for patrons only).
Public Transport:	None serving Ennerdale.

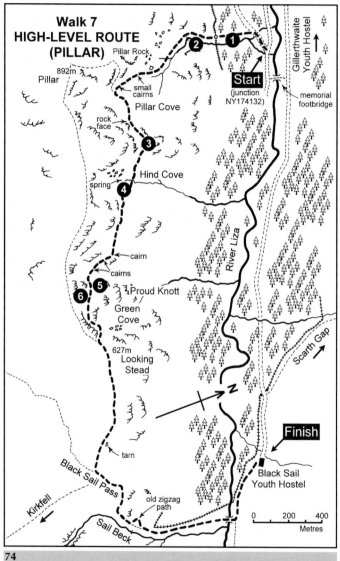

Walk 7
HIGH-LEVEL ROUTE
(PILLAR)

Pillar Rock

892m
Pillar

small cairns

Pillar Cove

rock face

3

Hind Cove

spring **4**

cairn

cairns

6 **5**

Proud Knott

Green Cove

627m
Looking Stead

tarn

Black Sail Pass

old zigzag path

Kirkfell

Sail Beck

2 **1**

Gillerthwaite Youth Hostel

Start
(junction NY174132)

memorial footbridge

River Liza

Scarth Gap

Z

Finish

Black Sail Youth Hostel

0   200   400
Metres

HIGH-LEVEL ROUTE (PILLAR)
SITE SUMMARY

1. **Pillar Ride (NY173130)**
   Mysterious white 'scratch-marks' found on mossy rock.

2. **Pillar's waterfall (NY172128)**
   Spectacular back-lighting of mist and spray when approaching from below.

3. **Robinson's Cairn (NY177124)**
   Memorial cairn and plaque built on hard volcanic intrusion. Veins of quartz with alpine flowers.

4. **Mountain spring (NY178122)**
   Water-source entering Hind Cove emerges from base of stone-chute producing a miniature fountain after heavy rainfall.

5. **Proud Knott (NY182118)**
   Fertile col with signs of ring ouzels. Territorial marking-stone used by foxes.

6. **Rock face (NY183117)**
   A variety of alpine plants including starry saxifrage and Alpine lady's-mantle.

wet day. But for the experienced hillwalker, properly equipped and not in a hurry, the mist and rain bring Pillar's north face to life. Savour the atmosphere – but don't rush it.

THE ROUTE

If you start at the Youth Hostel at Gillerthwaite, make your way 2 miles/3km up the valley along the forest roads until you reach the

junction at grid reference NY174132. Take the road that climbs up into the forest and look for the path (marked with an arrow) going steeply up through a gap in the trees on your left. Wainwright calls this the 'Pillar Ride' (see *The Western Fells*; Pillar, 13).

After approximately 330ft/100m, you will come to a prominent boulder slightly left of the path. You are now at **site 1**. There has been something strange about this rock ever since you noticed it at a distance. In a scene that is uniformly dark, it is the white patches that first catch the eye. Now that you are standing in front of it, the patches look like areas that have been scraped clean of their mossy covering. Walking poles, perhaps? – but there are no accompanying scratches on the stone surface and there are no tell-tale signs that the moss has been torn off by a stick.

A careful examination of the patches reveals that the moss simply has not grown over them. Pollution, perhaps from chemicals seeping out of the rock? – but the pattern is too regular. To solve the mystery it needs to be raining... and then you see the raindrops! They land precisely on the same spots time after time. This particular rock has its vertical face aligned exactly along the radial axis of an overhead pine so that water dripping from one of its branches continuously hits the rock at exactly the same spot. For this to produce the growth pattern in the moss it means that it rains here a lot and, more surprisingly, most of the time when it is raining – it isn't windy.

The narrow ride ends at a rowan where a rocky scramble to the left emerges into a clearing of bilberry and young forestry trees. This leads to the boundary fence where the path crosses an awkward stile onto the open fell.

Now the full scale of Pillar Rock can be seen up ahead and if the mist is swirling around this side of the valley, its dark shape is held in bold relief against the grey backdrop. The foreground is just as spectacular and totally unexpected. Here is one of the finest waterfalls in Lakeland. It is unnamed and there is no reference made to it on the OS map.

Make your way up towards the right-hand side of the main waterfall (**site 2**). If you are fortunate on your approach, and the sun shines through the mist, water appears to shoot out of the rocks above and the rising spray is lit up from behind. The walk is worth doing if only to capture this one scene on film.

The path becomes difficult as you make your way past smooth slabs and loose scree but after some scrambling, the gradient eases and you find yourself walking over grassy slopes covered in bilberry and alpine flowers. Almost everywhere you tread, there is Alpine lady's-mantle.

Keep to the right side of the beck even after it splits into its two tributaries in Pillar Cove. At this point you pass a number of large boulders and the faint path makes its way over increasingly steeper ground. After passing two **small cairns**, aim diagonally up left to join a narrow stony path. You are now on the High-Level Route.

Alpine lady's-mantle below Pillar Rock

After an initial drop, the path gently rises to pass close to a **rock face** with samples of fir club-moss. Down below, the ground drops away to Pillar Cove. Cross a level section of scree and boulders before climbing steadily for about 330ft/100m to reach Robinson's Cairn (**site 3**). You are now standing on the hard volcanic intrusion that separates Pillar Cove from Hind Cove. The view back to Pillar Rock and across to upper Ennerdale is magnificent. Drop down a few metres north below the cairn to see the brass plaque commemorating John Wilson Robinson. Notice the two parallel veins of quartz to its right. They follow a geological fault-line running north-west to south-east. For the next 160ft/50m the path is littered with rock shot-through with similar glistening white veins, some of which assume incredibly complex patterns. Just above the fault line is an area of fertile sandy gravel and where the path follows the fault it becomes a lawn of alpine flowers.

The path now drops steadily for about 2600ft/800m. The alpines disappear and the rock becomes a uniform brown colour where beds of sandstone appear within the volcanic lava. Follow the path into an open level area where a **spring** emerges from the base of a stone-chute. You are now at **site 4**. Take some time to trace this emerging stream. Alongside the path, the running water disappears under a large flat rock. If there has been heavy rain, it reappears immediately on the other side as a water fountain! It then disappears once more before going over the edge down a narrow gully. Notice the patches of rose-root on the gully sides.

After 1300ft/400m, the path drops before climbing to a **cairn**. At this point it bears right along the cliff edge. This difficult section is marked by a series of **cairns** leading to a steep downward scramble. Look for a solitary dwarf rowan alongside the path before climbing gently to a grassy spur.

You have now reached the top of a second arête known as **Proud Knott** (**site 5**). Like Robinson's Cairn, its foundation is volcanic ash, but here it is overlaid with fertile deposits of sandy gravel. Suddenly, every-where looks greener. Walk to the edge of the spur and look where the rocks on the cliff edge break through the grass. The top of each rock is covered in yellow lichen and the surrounding grass is dark-green. Take a closer look at the grass and notice what look like tiny worm-casts. They are in fact bird-droppings from a type of mountain thrush called a ring ouzel. This spur is its regular 'lookout perch' and the plantlife along its edge reflects the increased nitrogen left here.

Return from the spur to the path. A single boulder (shaped like a flat pyramid) occupies the highest point of this grassy col. Its position is strategically important for the local fox population. Look carefully and notice how the surrounding grass is dark green and left ungrazed by the sheep. On most visits here you will see fox-droppings. Sometimes you may detect the fox's scent left as a territorial marker.

The path continues around the rim of the next cove, appropriately named **Green Cove**. After passing a rowan tree it rises gently for 160ft/50m before levelling out next to a rock face covered in black moss (**site 6**). Here is a miniature alpine garden: starry saxifrage, oppo-site-leaved golden saxifrage, roseroot, two varieties of lady's-mantle, and a small rowan growing on top.

After this level section, the path drops briefly before climbing steeply for 330ft/100m. Notice the insectivorous butterworts growing

Looking down the Ennerdale Valley from Great Gable – Pillar Rock can be seen jutting out on the skyline to the right of Pillar's summit
(© Heather Lyon)

all along the right-hand side. The path then becomes a rocky switch-back for the next 980ft/300m involving some steep rock scrambling before joining the green spur that signals the end of the High-Level Route.

Join the main path from the Pillar ridge and drop back down into Ennerdale via **Black Sail Pass**.

Where the path approaches the cascades of **Sail Beck**, instead of following the badly eroded line alongside the water's edge, look for the **old zigzag path** leading diagonally left from one rowan to another. This original section is hardly ever trodden as it zigzags left and then right to join the 'new' path below the waterfalls. The old cairns can still be seen, but the sunken pathway is completely grassed over.

Continue on down through the glacial moraines to reach the youth hostel at **Black Sail Hut**. The perfect place to end a perfect day!

Walk 8

DALEGARTH

Stanley Ghyll is the perfect place for a wet day. It is sheltered and there is enough to see at close quarters to take your mind off the heaviest rainfall. Its main claim to fame is its variety of ferns, some of which grow only here and nowhere else in Cumbria.

The waterfall has a reputation as being the most beautiful in the Lake District. You could imagine entering a Himalayan jungle surrounded by exotic ferns and rhododendrons. The ravine gets narrower and more overgrown as you approach the upper falls, eventually reaching a chasm with 160ft/50m high vertical cliffs on each side.

Long after the Victorians came here to sample its 'terrors', the Outward Bound Mountain School at Eskdale used this area as a training ground. Up until the 1990s, a series of challenges were provided in and around the ghyll to test the leadership and initiative of trainees attending the school. The area is now rarely used but the signs still exist if you know where to look.

Most of the walks featured in this book involve some element of countryside interpretation concentrating on plant and animal life. This walk is more about tracing the activity of people. At times it becomes a 'whodunit?', as the search for clues recalls the history of Outward Bound at Eskdale.

THE ROUTE

Start at the Trough House Bridge **car park** and follow the lane leading up towards **Dalegarth Hall**. Turn left through a gate and follow the path until you reach another gate in the wall on your left. This is **site 1**. It is just an ordinary wooden gate in a stone wall. But take a close look at the stones on each side of the opening. Look at an area about 1.5ft/0.5m up from the ground. Notice the different lichens growing

CHECKLIST

Distance:	1 mile/1.6km.
Ascent:	260ft/80m.
Approximate Time:	1 hour.
Maps:	1:25 000 OS Outdoor Leisure 6, The English Lakes, South Western area.
Terrain:	Gentle woodland paths with one narrow muddy section when skirting around the top of the ghyll.
Degree of Shelter:	Very sheltered throughout.
Stiles:	One.
Special Considerations:	Take care with small children when approaching the platforms used for the 'Tyrolean Traverse'.
Footwear:	Boots are recommended (because of the section after crossing the stile above the ghyll).
Parking:	Public car parks at Dalegarth railway station (NY174007) and Trough House Bridge (NY172003).
Public Transport:	Trains from Ravenglass to Dalegarth (telephone 01229 717171 for timetable).

here. They are bright yellow, just as you would expect on the top of a wall enriched with bird-droppings – only this is at ground level. Perhaps there is a nest in the wall just above? But this is unlikely as you are at a busy crossroads where people stop to pass through the gate. The secret lies with these yellow lichens thriving on high levels of nitrogen, from *any* source. To discover the source – watch your dog as you approach the wall!

Continue on past the gate following the direction of the signpost to Stanley Ghyll and Birker Fell. Go through the next gate on your left to join the network of paths leading to the waterfall. When you reach the junction in front, take the right-hand path which climbs gently alongside the edge of the beck. A **plank footbridge** takes you across a dried-

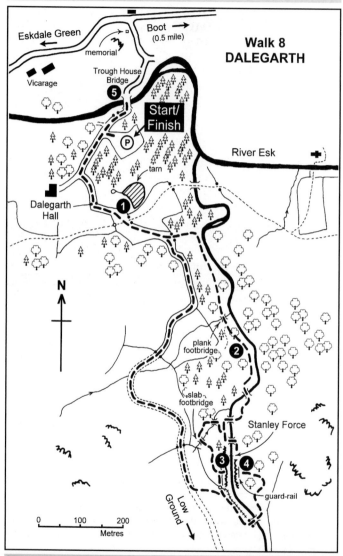

Eskdale Green

Boot →
(0.5 mile)

**Walk 8
DALEGARTH**

memorial

Vicarage

Trough House
Bridge

5

Start/
Finish

P

tarn

1

Dalegarth
Hall

River Esk

N

plank
footbridge

2

slab
footbridge

Stanley Force

3

4

guard-rail

Low
Ground
↓

0   100   200
Metres

DALEGARTH
SITE SUMMARY

1. **Gate in stone wall (NY172001)**
   Busy junction for walkers where the growth of
   lichen reflects the behaviour of their dogs.

2. **Shaded rock face (SD174998)**
   A variety of ferns including one of Britain's
   smallest species - Wilson's filmy fern.

3. **Rock platform viewpoint (SD174995)**
   Site of the 'Tyrolean Traverse' of Stanley Ghyll.
   Various clues remain that show how the crossing
   was made.

4. **East-side viewing platform (SD174995)**
   Cryptic message carved on guard-rail holds the
   secret of the ghyll crossing?

5. **Trough House Bridge (NY172004)**
   Site of the Outward Bound Mountain School's
   legendary 'bridge jump'.

up stream bed where there are patches of herb robert and yellow
pimpernel. You pass a large oak on your left after which the ghyll sides
start to get closer and begin to tower above the path (**site 2**). Notice
the fine specimens of hard fern on the rock wall above you. Its fertile
leaves resemble a fish's backbone. This is also a good place to find one
of the smallest of the British ferns – Wilson's filmy fern – so small it
could be mistaken for a moss.

Cross the first of three wooden footbridges. As the walls of the ghyll
sides continue to get closer, the atmosphere gets damper. Cross the
second footbridge. Everywhere you look there are ferns. Even the large

*Trough House Bridge where Outward Bound students
took their dip in the river*

oak on your left is covered in polpody, an aerial fern growing high up
on its branches.

To see **Stanley Force** waterfall, you need to cross the third footbridge and climb the rock steps to a viewpoint. In recent years, a land-
slip has made further progress difficult and there are signs warning
against approaching closer to the fall.

Retrace your steps across the third footbridge and then look for a
path leading off to the left. After negotiating a fallen tree, climb a series
of rock steps, first crossing and then keeping alongside a small tributary. Where the path levels out and comes to a junction, take the left
fork and cross a small stone-slab 'bridge'. After 130ft/40m, the path
swings right into an area that is relatively clear of vegetation. You may
find small piles of logs left in the remaining undergrowth. This is all
that is left of the rhododendrons that were cleared by students of the
Outward Bound School in the mid-80s. The rhododendrons are
regarded as a 'pest species' that are so vigorous they have to be pulled
out to give the native oaks a chance to regenerate.

The path now crosses some duck-boards and climbs a series of
wooden sleeper-steps before reaching a gap in a line of old iron rail-

ings. Alongside the gap is a 'Danger' sign warning of the 150ft drop in front of you at the 'Rock Platform Viewpoint'. This is **site 3** – and it's here that things start to get interesting!

The first thing you notice is the magnificent Scots pine towering above the rock platform. Take care and approach the edge to look down over the narrow ravine. If you are like most visitors at this stage, you will most likely be laid on your front with hands flat down and fingers hooked over the edge. Almost everyone who has visited this platform for the past 100 years has done just that. If you look at the edge you will see a bare strip of rock four inches wide (the average width of a palm) that has been rubbed clear of moss and lichen. In a fearful situation, a person's grip takes a very precise position.

There is much more to this site than at first appears, for this is where the Outward Bound School set one of its challenges known as the 'Tyrolean Traverse'. You had to get your team across the ravine using climbing rope and a length of fine string. Sometimes you had access to a few extras such as a catapult, and material for a small parachute.

How was it done? Well, the clues are still here but they need looking for. You need to look for anything unusual left behind after 50 years of attempted crossings. There must be some signs left on the rocks or on the trees or fences or somewhere. And that means looking carefully on *both* sides of the ravine.

If you look first to the right of the viewing platform you will see a birch tree growing on the edge. One of its branches juts out over the cliff below. Look at the junction of this branch with the main trunk and you will see a smoothly worn-out groove where an abseil rope has been anchored. Now look closely at the Scots pine at the back of the rock platform. At 3ft/1m and at 6.5ft/2m up from the ground there are faint traces of parallel rope burns sloping down towards the opposite side.

You now need to look for evidence on the opposite side of the ravine. To get there, follow the path alongside the iron railings to a stile that takes you outside the woodland and onto the open fell. The path follows the wire fence and crosses the wooden footbridge above the falls. Once over the bridge, the route climbs a short distance away from the beck before dropping down and returning back towards it. This section is narrow and muddy with exposed tree roots. Suddenly you find yourself looking across to the opposite viewing platform. You are separated from the drop in front by a wooden **guard-rail** and surrounded by rhododendrons (**site 4**). Notice the area of ground you are standing on has been covered at some time with granite chippings to make conditions drier for the groups attempting to cross.

There is something unusual about the guard-rail. If you look at the top plank you will see some strange figures carved neatly on its surface. Could this be a cryptic message that holds the key to crossing the ravine? Suddenly it feels like you've stepped into an Indiana Jones film!

The figures are difficult to make out but if you start from the left and work your way across you will see the four Roman numerals, 1 to 4, each one followed by an arrow pointing in a different direction. Four important steps that need to be taken in sequence to complete the task, perhaps?

So how *was* it done? First, the rope needs to be taken across (this is

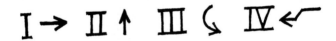

the difficult bit). It's just within throwing distance if the wind is favourable. Some groups attached the climbing rope to the fine string with a weight on the end and tried throwing it. Others used a catapult. Some have even tried to drift the thread across by parachute. Inevitably the thread became tangled in the small birch trees growing out from under the viewing platform and someone had to abseil down to retrieve it.

Once the first rope was across it had to be firmly attached. On one side, the Scots pine was used, but it was essential to attach the rope high up to allow for it stretching when loaded. On the other side, multiple attachments were used including the birch tree a few metres back from where you are now standing (look for suggestions of rope grooves at its base).

The first rope was followed by a second and a sliding transporter was then arranged so that it could be pulled back and forth along the double ropes. All that remained was to load up with each team member in turn and pull them across. And there you have it – the 'Tyrolean Traverse' of Stanley Ghyll.

*Dalegarth Force,
regarded by many as
the most beautiful
waterfall in the Lake
District*

After that, the rest of the walk seems like an anticlimax, but the Outward Bound has yet another surprise in store...

Return to the stile above site 3 and follow an indistinct path across the open fell to join the track from Low Ground back to Dalegarth Hall. Continue along the farm track (past the **car park** where you started) until you reach the River Esk at **Trough House Bridge** (**site 5**).

After the rope-crossing of Stanley Ghyll, the cool water below Trough House Bridge looks inviting. This is where Outward Bound students took a dip in the river, jumping from the top of the bridge! You can see the exact place where they jumped (where all the lichens have been worn away). Some of their initials can be found carved on the parapet and wood fence on the same side.

The story told is that it all started in the 50s. An instructor was taking his group of students for what is known as a 'quiet walk' – a part of the course where you were taken on a gentle walk on the first day to introduce you to the surrounding countryside. As he reached the top of the bridge he said 'follow me', and jumped over the side, fully clothed and still carrying his rucksack! The students simply followed.

Walk 9

TILBERTHWAITE GILL

This beautiful tree-lined ravine complete with its hidden water-falls has been a favourite with tourists for many years. Former guidebook writers describe magnificent gill scenery and recall how the upper ravine could be reached using a network of ladders and bridges. Although access to these upper reaches is now difficult (the ladders and bridges have long been swept away), Tilberthwaite Gill has many features that can still be explored.

At first glance it seems like a popular Sunday afternoon stroll. Then you hear the rock climbers and see the cavers with their miner's lamps and underground maps and you realise that there is more to this place than just the scenery.

This is the perfect walk for a wet day. There is enough here to concentrate your eyes downwards and to make you forget the mist-covered tops. And if the sun does happen to shine – the scenery is magnificent!

THE ROUTE

From the **car park** at Low Tilberthwaite climb a series of slate steps that leads up the side of a large heap of **quarry spoil**. Notice the large number of foxgloves that have colonised these loose piles of stone. Even the sheep know that these plants are poisonous and leave them well alone. Soon the path branches off to the left into a large **quarry cave**. In wet weather this is a good place to shelter.

Continue along the main path until you reach the first of three side-entrances that lead into **Penny Rigg Quarry**. Turn off left at the first entrance. You are now standing at the foot of the quarry. Directly ahead of you is the north-facing quarry wall – a vertical rock face with a rowan tree on top (**site 1**).

Here is a puzzle. Directly below the tree is a band of grey, leafy lichen called crottle. Normally these lichens would grow in circular

CHECKLIST

Distance:	1.5 miles/2.4km.
Ascent:	620ft/190m.
Approximate Time:	1 to 1.5 hours.
Maps:	1:25 000 OS Outdoor Leisure 6, The English Lakes, South Western area. 1:50 000 OS Landranger 96 and 97. 1:50 000 British Geological Survey, England and Wales Sheet 38, Ambleside.
Terrain:	Mostly well-defined paths. The approach to site 3 requires some care.
Degree of Shelter:	Sheltered from strong winds along lower sections. Shelter from heavy rain possible in some of the quarry caves and tunnel entrances.
Stiles:	None.
Special Considerations:	Try to avoid causing erosion of the gill sides when approaching and leaving site 3. Please do not pick or damage any of the lichens found on this route but leave them for others to enjoy. Unless you are properly equipped for caving and have appropriate experience, avoid exploring any of the adits or quarry tunnels.
Footwear:	Boots.
Parking:	Low Tilberthwaite car park (NY306010).
Public Transport:	Limited bus service to High Yewdale, 1 mile/1.6km from Low Tilberthwaite car park (Stagecoach; summer service 506 from Coniston to Skelwith Bridge).

colonies, like mould on top of a jar of jam. Look closely at these particular colonies. None of them is circular. All that is left of the circular
shapes are spindly crescents – the lower edges having been 'eaten
away'.

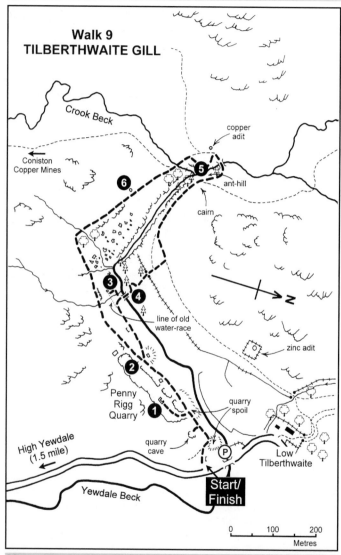

Walk 9
TILBERTHWAITE GILL

Crook Beck

Coniston
Copper Mines

copper
adit

6

5

ant-hill

cairn

3

4

line of old
water-race

zinc adit

2

Penny
Rigg
Quarry

1

quarry
spoil

High Yewdale
(1.5 mile)

quarry
cave

Low
Tilberthwaite

Yewdale Beck

Start/
Finish

0   100   200
Metres

TILBERTHWAITE GILL
SITE SUMMARY

1. **Quarry wall (NY306009)**
   Why are the circular lichen colonies underneath the rowan 'eaten away' along their lower edges?

2. **Quarry entrance (NY305008)**
   Diameter of lichen colony reveals the date when quarry was last operating.

3. **Tunnel entrance (NY303006)**
   170ft/52m rock tunnel for diverting water via water-race to Penny Rigg Quarry.

4. **Bank of vegetation (NY303007)**
   Interesting group of ferns and lichens including a 'horizontal' dog lichen.

5. **Viewpoint (NY299008)**
   Rocky knoll with view of waterfall.

6. **Copper adit (NY301006)**
   Tunnel entrance showing growth of trees on top where sheep grazing has been restricted.

What is happening here? It may be significant that this area of volcanic rock contains soluble metals and that this particular quarry face has many seepage cracks. It may also be significant that lichen colonies growing on vertical surfaces hold onto water like a dripping sponge. It is interesting that this pattern of lichen growth is only seen on sloping or vertical surfaces.

Retrace your steps out of the quarry and continue along the main

A wet October morning at Low Tilberthwaite – the spoil-heap from Penny Rigg Quarry can be seen on the right

path for a short distance to the second entrance. Notice the rowan tree on the right-hand side of this rock-cutting. The rock is being split vertically by the roots as they grow along the cleavage plane and expand sideways.

Continue on to the third entrance (**site 2**). On the right-hand side of the rock passage is a white circle with a radius of 70mm. This is a colony of slow-growing lichen that adds on average just 0.5mm of fresh growth to its radius each year. Look carefully and you should see the concentric growth-rings around its outer margin. By measuring the largest colony you can work out a rough date for when this quarry entrance was cut through. A 70mm radius growing at 0.5mm a year means that it started growing on this freshly cut rock about 140 years ago! This ties in with the date when the quarry was believed to have closed in 1875.

Continue along the main path to a junction. Take the right-hand branch that follows closely the south bank of the gill. You pass a wooden seat ('In memory of Charles Eric Samsom 1946–1965') from where you can see the footbridge spanning the tree-lined gorge. The path you are now following was the **line of the old water-race** that supplied power to the machinery in Penny Rigg Quarry.

Stop where the path turns right (where it leads down to a set of steep steps). At this point the water-race would have continued on up ahead in a straight line along the gillside. Strangely, it is heading higher up the gill along a course which is far too high to collect water from this section of Yewdale Beck. From where you are standing, the source of the quarry water is still a mystery.

For the moment, follow the footpath down the steps towards the wooden footbridge. There are some splendid mosses alongside these steps indicating that the air is getting progressively wetter. Most have brush-like leaves and belong to a group of mosses known as *Polytrichum* (which means 'many hairs').

Once you arrive at the footbridge and before crossing, drop down to the left-hand side and follow a narrow path between rocks and loose scree. This is a botanist's paradise with yellow saxifrage and herb robert growing at eye-level. After walking 130ft/40m from the footbridge, turn left up a steep bank. This is loose soil and scree that has been partially covered by various grasses and herbs. Look up at this point and you will see a low rock bar extending down on your right. Make your way towards this, taking care to avoid any further erosion by carefully zigzagging upwards. The bar of rock is a natural rock garden with wood sorrel, yellow saxifrage and wild strawberries. It is here, 33ft/10m up from the waterside path, that you find the secret of the quarry's water supply.

Below a rowan is the entrance to a rock tunnel (**site 3**) that extends nearly 170ft/52m in a straight line beneath the south bank of the gill to collect water from the upper reaches of Yewdale Beck. Although this tunnel has been described as 'safe enough', it is not recommended to venture too far along its length unless you have the proper caving equipment. It is however an excellent shelter in wet weather and once inside the entrance looking back out, you can sight the line of the old water-race and see how its gentle gradient lines up exactly with the path alongside the memorial seat.

From the tunnel, retrace your steps carefully back to the footbridge and cross over to the other side. Notice the bank of vegetation immediately facing you (**site 4**) with samples of herb robert, maidenhair spleenwort and a very interesting plant with smooth, shiny leaves coloured greeny-grey with patches of pale brown. The leaf edges have projecting discs that have an uncanny resemblance to the starship *Enterprise*! This is another form of dog lichen (*Peltigera horizontalis*) but the exciting thing about this species is that it is described by botanists as an 'old forest indicator'. It is found in ancient forests but not in newly planted woodland. This would suggest that Tilberthwaite Gill has had a long and continuous history of tree cover.

Follow the path for a few metres until you reach a National Trust map showing the recent path alterations. At this point climb the steps to the right, taking you out of the gill. Go through the gate in the fence alongside a fine specimen of larch. The path now makes its way up through dense bracken until reaching the track that climbs above the northern edge of the gill.

If the weather is poor and time is pressing, an alternative route back to the car park can be made by turning right at this junction and following the track that leads past an old zinc mine, joining the road at Low Tilberthwaite. If you decide to continue your ascent around the head of the gill, turn left and follow the well-engineered path along the north edge of the gill.

There are spectacular views all along this section with an almost vertical drop on your left down into the ravine below. After passing a group of juniper, birch and larch growing up from the cliff walls, you get your first view of the waterfalls. The path continues past a **cairn** and then a quarry path that leads off to the right. Keep straight ahead. On the left are two windswept larches, a prominent **ant-hill** (yellow meadow ants) and two more larches before you reach a wooden foot-bridge.

Cross the bridge. Ahead of you (west of the bridge) there is an entrance to an old **copper adit** with a birch growing on top. Some shelter can be found here in heavy rain. The main path now crosses a water-logged area of peat. Do not follow this but take the narrow path that keeps close to the south bank of the beck. See if you can spot a dry rock in the middle of the path where bird-pellets can sometimes be found. Most of this section is very wet because of the surrounding peat. This is a good place to find the insectivorous butterwort and sundew.

The line taken by the beck along this section runs south-east from the footbridge in a straight line. This is a fault line that contains a rich vein of copper ore. The beck has cut a deep ravine along the fault which hides a fine waterfall in the gorge below. To see this at its best, continue along the path, past a group of birch and then an area of bracken. The path now drops down left to a narrow, rocky viewpoint (**site 5**).

Tilberthwaite Gill – the tunnel entrance at site 3

From this rocky knoll, climb away from the ravine along a wet corridor of rushes with bracken on either side. Join the main path that skirts around the top of the gill and cross the jumble of boulders over **Crook Beck**. The path now drops steadily down keeping above the south side of the gill with dramatic views on the left of the tree-lined gorge below.

Look for a prominent cairn on a grassy, level area on the left side of the path. This marks the site of another adit on the right (**site 6**). You may have noticed that most of the mine openings seen on this walk have trees growing directly on top. Perhaps these excavations have made it more difficult for sheep to graze here, allowing young trees to become established. This particular opening supports a rowan and several juniper.

At first the path follows a fairly level section with crags on the left covered in birch, ash and juniper. It then becomes more rocky, dropping down to cross a small stream. Eventually you rejoin the quarry path that takes you back to your starting point at the car park.

Walk 10

WALLOWBARROW AND GRASSGUARDS

Most valley roads follow the river – but not in Dunnerdale. Motorists leaving Seathwaite may think they are following the River Duddon but the road is forced to take a detour along the tributary of Tarn Beck. The main river valley makes its way through the Wallowbarrow Gorge which can only be entered on foot. This is a special place: of quiet rock pools, ancient stepping-stones and giant wood ants.

On a raised platform on the far side of this gorge is Grassguards – once known for its wool used in the manufacture of carpets and rugs. If you look across the valley from Walna Scar Road, the area stands out as a fertile pasture. But it is not until you get up close to this ancient homestead that you see the evidence of the skill and industry of its past inhabitants. A walk through Grassguards for the first time leaves a lasting impression. There are walls here that rank with the Celtic Brochs of Glenelg and the Chambered Cairns of Orkney – only their impact is all the greater for being totally unexpected.

THE ROUTE

Start at the **gate** opposite the 'School House' (signpost: 'Permitted Path, Wallowbarrow'). After crossing the concrete footbridge over Tarn Beck, follow the path straight ahead through an oak and birch woodland until you drop down to join the River Duddon. If the river level is low you will pass a flood channel along this section resembling a dried-up riverbed. When the river level is high, many of the trees along here are left stranded on their own narrow island.

Continue alongside the river until you reach the **stepping-stones** made famous by one of Wordsworth's sonnets. There are many stepping-stones across the Duddon but these are some of the oldest and

The Cockpit at Moor Divock (Walk 12)

The church of Saint Martin, Martindale (Walk 14) (© Heather Lyon)

Cladonia

Crottle

Dog lichen

Trametes versicolor

CHECKLIST

Distance:	3.5 miles/5.7km.
Ascent:	525ft/160m.
Approximate Time:	3 hours.
Maps:	1:25 000 OS Outdoor Leisure 6, The English Lakes, South Western area. 1:50 000 OS Landranger 96. 1:50 000 British Geological Survey, England and Wales Sheet 38, Ambleside.
Terrain:	Fairly gentle farm and forestry tracks. Some of the narrow woodland paths are steep and slippery in places.
Degree of Shelter:	Very sheltered throughout the woodland sections. Exposed on the forestry track from Low Stonythwaite to Grassguards.
Stiles:	Seven (for those wishing to walk with their dog, there are gates that may be used alongside most stiles).
Special Considerations:	Please keep to the path along the Wallowbarrow Gorge. Any routes on the crag above or below the path are dangerous and should be avoided.
Footwear:	Boots with good grip.
Parking:	There are a number of places where cars may pull off along the roadside north of Seathwaite Church (SD230963). Please note that parking outside the Newfield Inn is for patrons only.
Public Transport:	A post bus supplies the valley twice a day, Monday to Friday. There is also a limited Stagecoach service from Ulverston to Seathwaite (service 523).

probably date back to the 13th Century. Notice the alder tree to the right of the first stone. It is covered in bracket fungus.

About 33ft/10m further, between the path and the river edge, you

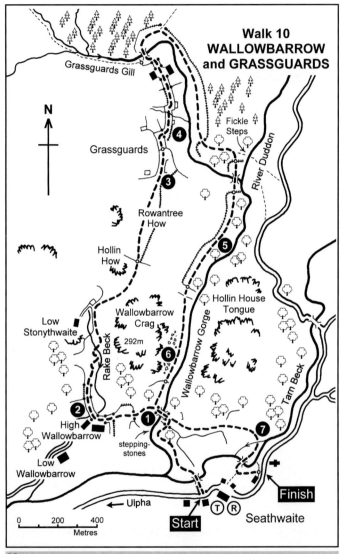

Walk 10
WALLOWBARROW
and GRASSGUARDS

Grassguards Gill

N

Fickle
Steps

River Duddon

Grassguards

④

③

Rowantree
How

Hollin
How

⑤

Low
Stonythwaite

Wallowbarrow
Crag

Hollin House
Tongue

Rake Beck

292m

⑥

Wallowbarrow Gorge

Tarn Beck

②

High
Wallowbarrow

①

⑦

Low
Wallowbarrow

stepping-
stones

✝

Finish

← Ulpha

0   200   400

Metres

Start

Ⓣ Ⓡ

Seathwaite

WALLOWBARROW AND GRASSGUARDS
SITE SUMMARY

1. **Memorial footbridge (SD224964)**
   Greek and Norwegian connections with carved signs and inscriptions.

2. **High Wallowbarrow Farm (SD221963)**
   Band of red microgranite seen in path and farm buildings.

3. **Grassguards' walls (SD224976)**
   Some of Lakeland's finest stone walls: 10ft/3m high, 13ft/4m thick! Fine specimens of lichen and moss.

4. **A fencepost puzzle (SD224978)**
   Why does no lichen grow below the top line of wire?

5. **Viewpoint (SD227973)**
   Raised clearing with views of Wallowbarrow Gorge.

6. **Boulder field (SD225967)**
   Heavy volcanic rocks resting on weak foundations. Aerial displays of ravens and peregrines.

7. **Weir and sluice-gate (SD229962)**
   Nearby water-wheel generated electricity for Seathwaite before valley was connected to the National Grid.

pass a mound of chewed-up leaves. If you look carefully, especially when the weather is warm, the leaves will appear to be moving. This is a nest made by the wood ant, *Formica lugubris*. These giant ants are thought to have invaded the Wallowbarrow woods after being introduced at Duddon Hall to feed pheasants. You don't want to be standing here too long!

The path leads on through a gate in a wall to **site 1**. This is the Memorial Bridge, mistakenly believed to be a memorial to the RAF. As you walk between its carefully constructed parapets, notice that the north-facing side supports a healthy growth of wall rue thriving on the lime-mortar. This shade-loving fern avoids the direct sunlight and struggles to grow on the drier south-facing side.

When you reach the middle of the span, look over the left side to see the initials A.B. carved on a stone plaque. Over on the opposite side, there is a mysterious rune-like carving that could almost have stepped out from a Tolkien story. On careful inspection, and allowing for the fact that you are looking at it upside down, you can see the Greek letters alpha and omega enclosing a star-shaped symbol.

Just before leaving the bridge, on the inside of the right-hand wall, there is another carved plaque: 'BUILT BY W. GRISENTHWAITE FOR A.F. AND R.A.F. 1934'.

'A.F.' was Aida Foster and 'R.A.F.' was a Greek scholar, Robert Allason Furness. They were respectively the daughter and friend of

'A.B.', Aida Borchgrevink (born Starr). Aida Starr had married a Norwegian and after the 1914–18 war lived in Duddon where she died in 1931. It sounds very complicated but look again at the carvings on the outside of the bridge. The Greek letters *alpha* and *omega* intertwined with a symbol of her maiden name was specifically chosen to commemorate A.B.'s life: beginning and ending as a 'star' in the eyes of her friends.

If the river is not in flood, turn right on crossing the bridge, and carefully make your way down to the water's edge to examine the underside of the arch. It has been constructed of cast concrete and the lime is slowly leaching out as the rainwater drips through. Notice the stalactites that are forming under the arch and the one small stalagmite developing at your feet where the arch joins the ground.

From the bridge take the woodland path leading west away from the river. After approximately 650ft/200m you reach a gate into open parkland where the path contours around a pleasant grassy terrace. Along this section look for the remains of birds killed by peregrines which take advantage of this open area to land with their prey.

Follow the waymarked path through several farm gates taking you past the gardens and exotic wildfowl of **High Wallowbarrow** (**site 2**). The red stones in some of the farm buildings come from an intrusion of red microgranite that extends north-east from here in a straight line parallel with the gorge. Keep to the farm track as it climbs steadily along the west bank of **Rake Beck** below the rock-climbing pitches of Wallowbarrow Crag. Once above the tree-line there are extensive views behind of the lower Duddon Valley.

Follow the track over the exposed fell passing **Low Stonythwaite** on your left. Try spotting the two vertical bands of quartz on **Hollin How**. The holly trees that gave it its name are not so obvious, but a little further along, the rowans of **Rowantree How** can still be found.

The track takes you on down into **Grassguards** (**site 3**). The first thing you notice are the walls. These are no ordinary walls. They reach heights of 10–13ft/3–4m and in places are 13ft/4m thick! They are beautifully constructed tapering towards the perfectly levelled coping-stones. Some appear to serve little function other than to act as a tidy store for stones cleared from the fields.

As you approach the entrance of this stone labyrinth, you face two birch trees standing like sentinels on each side. Drop down from the track below the right-hand tree where a drainage channel runs past the wall end. If you have never taken an interest in lichen before, take some time here particularly if it's wet. Look at the corner foundation stone. It is covered in rock tripe: groups of greeny-grey leaves attached by a single cord to the rock, their undersurface covered in holes just like tripe. In the Highlands of Scotland these plants were used for dying wool after being boiled and treated with urine to produce the most delicate shades of mauve. Alongside is a type of cup lichen. The thin stems and scarlet tips resemble bunches of twisted matchsticks.

Continue around this harbour-like wall to rejoin the path. The side facing the sun is covered in what could be a map of Europe: separate countries painted bright yellow, their borders outlined in black together with their towns and cities. This is map lichen. Notice the flattened shape of the 'countries' and how they follow the grain in the volcanic rock (quite different from the shapes found on Eskdale Granite where there is no regular grain to follow).

As you cross the ladder-stile, you are able to look down on the tops of these walls. The coping-stones are covered in a type of moss that is normally found on exposed mountain tops. This plant is a good indicator of humidity and can predict a forthcoming change in weather conditions. The side facing a drying wind turns from green to grey as the leaf tips are transformed into hoary-white wisps. This distinctive appearance gives it the name: frizzy-hair moss.

After turning right through a gate, you enter a more open area with a wire fence on one side (**site 4**). Lichens are extremely sensitive to pollution, particularly from metals like zinc and iron. Look at the fence-posts where the galvanised wire has been stapled to the wood. Lichen thrives on the top but immediately below the first line of wire, where the zinc and iron have drained down, the wood is clear of all growth – as if it has been scraped clean. One of the best examples can be seen in front of you – on the seventh post back from the stone ruin.

Continue on past the farmhouses and turn left at the ford to cross the footbridge. Once over the bridge, the path leads to a gate. Don't go through the gate but turn right following the sign: 'Coast to Coast Cycle Route'. The path drops gently at first following the line of **Grassguards Gill**. After a gate in the fence, the way becomes steeper involving a tricky descent over wet and slippery rock (do cyclists actually cycle this?). The atmosphere gets progressively wetter and darker as you enter a mature beech wood and eventually you reach the gorge in what seems like perpetual twilight. In front of you are the notoriously **Fickle Steps** complete with wire hand-rail. Be warned! – if you are planning to cross the river at this point after a period of heavy rain, these stepping-stones can be impassable. The water level can rise very quickly particularly if held back by a high tide in the Duddon estuary – an effect that is increased during a westerly gale.

Your route keeps to the west bank of the **River Duddon** along the foot of the gorge. Cross the fence at the stile. Notice the bracken leaves trapped in the wire on your left showing the level of the river when it's in flood. Continue over the footbridge and then over a boggy section with duck-boards.

Ravens flying above Wallowbarrow Gorge

You are surrounded by bog myrtle and enclosed by trees. Eventually the path climbs as it follows the line of the fence. Look for a dry bracken-covered mound on the left (**site 5**). *Take care here: the rising path is indistinct.* This provides a good vantage point to view the other side of the gorge.

The path crosses a boggy area and then a small stream before dropping steeply. This section is narrow with exposed tree roots and requires care when wet. The yellow flower along the side of the path is cow-wheat.

A.B.'s Memorial Bridge over the River Duddon

After crossing a stile and then a gap in a broken wall, the path crosses a line of block-scree along the foot of **Wallowbarrow Crag**. The views up towards the towering cliffs and pinnacles are dramatic and in summer you will hear the alarm calls of peregrines and ravens as they compete for space in the air above.

As you progress across the scree, the boulders get larger, some providing a welcome shelter under their leaning faces (**site 6**). What has caused this jumble of fallen rock and why has it developed on this side of the gorge and not on the other? Both sides of the gorge are made of andesite larva but here on the west bank there is a weaker layer of sandstone sandwiched between the denser volcanics. The combination of heavy rock resting on a weak foundation causes an unstable cliff face. Andesite splits along three planes, each at right angles to the other, and so it breaks into the rectangular-shaped boulders that you see in front of you.

After crossing a broken wall, the path becomes much easier and leads back through the woods to the Memorial footbridge. Cross the bridge and follow the path straight ahead, keeping the wall on your right. The path leads across an open boggy area and brings you back to Tarn Beck (**site 7**). The small weir across the beck was built along with the sluice-gate and water-channel to redirect the flow to a horizontal water-wheel. The electricity generated supplied the nearby inn and farm buildings before the valley was connected to the 'mains' in 1951.

Follow the beck and cross over the wooden footbridge into a grassy field (notice on the right the low outcrop of volcanic rock that has been smoothed and polished by glacial action). Bear left and follow the sign to Seathwaite Church, finally making your way through a stone gap-stile to join the valley road.

If you have time, visit the Newfield Inn to see a particularly fine example of flow-banded slate that came from the Walna Scar Quarries. It was used in the flag-stone floors of the public bar and in many of the nearby houses. The pattern of complex parallel banding is unique to the Duddon Valley.

Walk 11

AIRA FORCE

Seasoned walkers of the Lakeland fells may dismiss Aira Force as an artificial 'pleasure garden' that is best left to families with prams or car-bound tourists wishing to stretch their legs. Think again – especially on a wet day.

Even if there was nothing else to see but the waterfall, this walk would leave a lasting impression. It is busy and there are families (but not with prams) and the paths and steps are artificial; but the first time you see Aira Force, the cynicism disappears. Even the purist must admire the bridges.

Stand behind the iron rails looking up to where the main fall shoots under the top bridge and the clichés are forgiven. The view is literally breath-taking! The sheer volume of water pouring 70ft/21m into a confined space causes air to be displaced sideways and upwards. The spray is forced out to meet you and the noise is deafening. If there are rainbows, the first colour will be orange, reflecting the small size of the water droplets found in the swirling mist.

Coming face to face with such elemental forces is all the more 'shocking' following an approach that has been so contrived. You are led to expect a Victorian water-garden where nature has been tamed and put on display. But in effect, the ordered paths and exotic trees serve merely to highlight the savagery that awaits you!

THE ROUTE

This walk begins at one of the busiest **car park**s in the district. Choose a wet day and if you are arriving by car in the height of the season, arrive early morning or evening to guarantee a place.

Make your way through the gap alongside the **National Trust Information** building. Follow the iron railings and pass through the

CHECKLIST

Distance:	1.4 miles/2.3km.
Ascent:	260ft/80m.
Approximate Time:	1 hour.
Maps:	1:25 000 OS Outdoor Leisure 5, The English Lakes, North Western area.
Terrain:	Well-maintained footpaths and steps throughout the entire walk.
Degree of Shelter:	Excellent shelter from wind, rain and sun.
Stiles:	None.
Special Considerations:	The ideal walk for a wet day.
Footwear:	Ordinary shoes or trainers.
Parking:	National Trust car park (NY401201).
Public Transport:	Buses connecting Penrith and Patterdale (Stagecoach; service 108, at least one bus every 2 hours at least six days a week).

gate with the National Trust's acorn emblem on each side. The broad path has a wire fence on the right, behind which is a fine specimen of one of Lakeland's native hardwoods – the durmast or sessile oak.

Look closely at the wire fence at the corner where there is a gate and square gateposts (**site 1**). Notice the lichens. This is where wet conditions are an advantage, for when it's wet these plants swell up and change colour becoming more obvious. The wooden posts in front of you are covered in lichen, especially their tops. But what looks like a haphazard distribution turns out to be a complex study in ecology.

On closer inspection you begin to notice that the healthy growth on the top of each post is suddenly cut off a few inches down – exactly where the fence wire is wrapped around the square posts. The same bare pattern can be seen immediately below the rusted hinges on the gate. Iron and zinc kill lichen and where the oxides have run down into the wood there is nothing growing. Look back along the line of wooden posts that you have just passed and in particular look at the first post back from the corner. The top staple is all that is needed to stop the lichens spreading below!

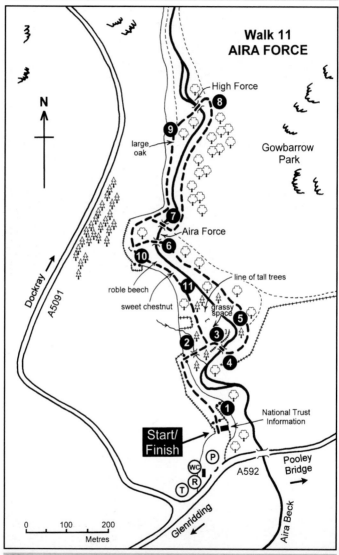

Walk 11
AIRA FORCE

High Force

8

9

large oak

Gowbarrow Park

N

7

Aira Force

6

10

line of tall trees

roble beech

11

sweet chestnut

grassy space

5

2

3

4

1

National Trust Information

Start/ Finish

P

wc

T R

A592

Pooley Bridge

Dockray

A5091

Glenridding

Aira Beck

0   100   200
Metres

AIRA FORCE – SITE SUMMARY

1. **Wire fence (NY401202)**
   Effect of metal-poisoning on lichens caused by rusty iron wire.

2. **Grand fir (NY400203)**
   Unusual fir with large leaves that smell of oranges.

3. **Tall tree viewpoint (NY401203)**
   Chilean pine, Himalayan fir, Douglas fir and silver fir can be seen looking north across grassy clearing.

4. **Monterey pine (NY401203)**
   Unusual pine with needles in groups of three.

5. **Sitka spruce (NY401204)**
   One of the largest specimens in Britain with a circumference of over 20ft/6m.

6. **Lower stone bridge (NY399205)**
   View of Aira Force. Hart's-tongue fern growing on bridge masonry.

7. **Upper stone bridge (NY399206)**
   View looking down onto Aira Force.

8. **High Force (NY401208)**
   Narrow rock channel spanned by wooden footbridge.

9. **Alder tree (NY400208)**
   Old specimen attacked by woodpeckers, fungi and a parasitic rowan.

10. **Viewpoint (NY399205)**
    Views of Place Fell over boundary wall.

11. **Silver fir (NY400204)**
    The tallest tree in Cumbria at a height of 160ft/50m.

Continue on the broad path and pass through the gate in a stone wall. Suddenly it becomes darker as you enter a Victorian arboretum. There are two yew trees, one on each side of the path and then the first large conifer is seen on the left (**site 2**). To the left of a wooden balcony and a fallen hollow trunk is a tall evergreen named grand fir (*Abies grandis*). Everything about this tree is big. The leaves are like those of a Christmas tree only four times larger. When bruised they smell of oranges.

Cross the bridge and follow the path to the right around the edge of an open **grassy space** and stand at the gap in the low wooden fence (**site 3**). In front of you across the grass about 330ft/100m away is a line of some of Lakeland's tallest trees. Starting on the left you will probably recognise the monkey-puzzle tree or Chilean pine (*Araucaria araucana*). To its right and behind is the much rarer Himalayan fir (*Abies spectabilis*); then the tallest in the group, a Douglas fir (*Pseudotsuga menziesii*). The next tall tree on the right is the European silver fir (*Abies alba*) and the group finally ends with another monkey-puzzle tree. (Incidentally, if you really want to impress (or lose!) your friends, the scientific name of the Douglas fir is taken from the surname of the Scot who discovered it and is pronounced 'mingiz-i-eye'.)

After some steps and crossing a bridge over the river you will find a young pine to the right of the path (**site 4**). This is a Monterey pine (*Pinus radiata*). Although it is very sensitive to frosts, it is one of the most wind-resistant pines, helped by the extremely wide spacing of its needles.

Now the path begins to climb up a series of steps and bears left. Just before the path forks to the right, you pass an old ash with wood-pecker holes. Keep left and you will come face to face with a real giant and one of the most remarkably shaped trees in the Lake District (**site 5**). Here is a Sitka spruce (*Picea sitchensis*) with a circumference of over 20ft/6m, making it one of the largest specimens in the British Isles. (The largest is in Devon with a circumference of 27ft/8m.) At some stage, a side branch grew out horizontally and then decided to grow vertically like the spout of an up-turned coffee pot. On a smaller side-branch just above the path, you will see a bird's nest.

A few metres further down from the path is another giant, this time a particularly fine specimen of silver fir, so-named because in sunshine the foliage has a silvery gleam due to white patches on the back of the needles. At this point you can almost be forgiven for forgetting the main reason for coming here – to see the waterfalls!

Continue along the path as it makes its way down past some large oaks with wood sage and cow-wheat along the path side. A series of steps takes you down to a stone bridge (**site 6**). You know something is different here from the noise and the fine mist in the air. Look over the right-hand parapet to see hart's-tongue fern and polypody growing on the bridge stonework, thriving in the perpetually damp air. As you leave the bridge, notice the patch of wild garlic just to the left of the path.

A few steps further and you arrive at the muddy viewing platform. **Aira Force** can now be seen pouring through the stone arch of a distant bridge spanning the narrow gorge.

Climb the steps and then bear round to the right to join the path that leads to the top bridge (**site 7**). As you look down directly over the fall, try spotting the honeysuckle growing amongst the rocks on the left.

After crossing the bridge, follow the path left along the east side of the river. After approximately 330ft/100m, at a bend in the river, the flowing water can be seen to have undercut the rock walls that enclose it. Continue along the path until you reach a wooden footbridge spanning a narrow rock channel. This is **High Force (site 8)**.

From the footbridge follow the path that runs between the west bank of the beck and an old boundary wall. After a few metres you will pass an alder tree (**site 9**). Look carefully at the trunk 3ft/1m up on the side facing the wall. It has a small, green plastic tab with the number 00150. This is a curious tree: an ancient alder with an alien rowan growing right through its middle. About 6.5ft/2m up the trunk on the path side, notice the holes left by a woodpecker looking for grubs. As if this wasn't enough, this troubled tree is also being attacked by a bracket fungus.

You now pass a line of three oaks on the left side of the path. All of them have polypody ferns growing high up on their branches. The third **oak** is massive and has been numbered by the National Trust. See if you can spot the green tab (number 00250).

The wall runs very close to the path along this section. The aspect is much brighter here due to the reduced tree cover and the lichens take full advantage of the extra light. Look for cup lichen all along this section of wall.

You pass more alder and some sycamore on your left and then the beck goes over a small waterfall. The ash that leans over it is covered in polypody. Your route takes you on (past the path that leads down to

Aira Force – ideal for a wet day (© Heather Lyon)

the stone bridge above Aira Force), now following the wire boundary fence. Continue on (past the junction down to the lower stone bridge) keeping straight ahead past the seat with a view of the Force. The view is getting progressively less each year due to the increasing foliage. Further along the path you have an unexpected view over a sheep-pen out over the boundary fence across to Place Fell (**site 10**). A boundary wall now replaces the fence (keep looking for cup lichen). After descending more steps, the path levels out. At this point, 10ft/3m to the left of the path, you will find an unusual southern-hemisphere tree – a **roble beech** (*Northofagus obliqua*) – introduced into Britain from Chile in 1902.

A little further and you pass a group of silver birch, two of which are leaning precariously over the wall, and then you pass a thicket of rhododendrons. The boundary wall now becomes low enough to look over. The green pasture outside is full of molehills indicating a rich fertile soil with plenty of earthworms. The growing conditions here are perfect and the huge trees that we are about to approach reflect this.

First we pass three **sweet chestnut** trees (*Castanea sativa*). The third one shows the plant's characteristic sign of old age. As it grows old, the bark cracks in a spiral pattern giving the impression that the trunk is turning anticlockwise as it gains height.

Alongside are two towering Christmas trees or Norway spruce (*Picea abies*) and then a little lower down towards the river edge is a silver fir (**site 11**). This tree is 160ft/50m high and is the tallest tree in Cumbria.

The path now drops gently and becomes very dark, passing a rectangular enclosure with yet another monkey-puzzle tree struggling for light. There is a group of yew on the left and 33ft/10m away from the path on the right is another roble beech almost hidden in the under-growth along with a specimen of grand fir that has recently fallen over but is still alive.

All that remains now is to join the path that leads around the edge of the **grassy space** and retrace your steps back to the car park.

Walk 12

MOOR DIVOCK

On a hot sunny day, I wasn't prepared for this. At times, I felt like an archaeologist exploring the tombs of Egypt complete with wide-brimmed sun hat and parasol. And then I was strolling down the wide fairway of what could have been a golf course complete with hidden bunkers. We are, of course, in the Lake District just a few miles out from Pooley Bridge, but this is totally unexpected.

Moor Divock is a Bronze Age site and most of what is here has been well documented. There are robbed burial cairns, stone circles, cairn circles, and standing stones. Archaeologists have also identified two parallel lines of stones – the Askham Fell Stone Alignment – used possibly for ceremonial purposes associated with the many funeral sites.

And then there are the 'shake-holes' – following definite lines like wartime bomb craters. At first you don't see them, and then you find one and you are drawn further on to the next, wondering how deep and if it will be full of water.

What makes this place different is that all this interest is hidden. When you set off walking from Roehead you wonder what all the fuss is about. There is nothing but flat open moorland. Even when you have reached the first signpost after half a mile, there is nothing. One more mile and still nothing. And then it begins…

WARNING

The moorland track from Roehead is wide and easy to follow but once you leave the track, there are no clear paths leading to the archaeological sites or shake-holes. Even when conditions are clear, great care is needed when searching for the described sites. Most of them cannot be seen until you are 'on top of them'.

It may help to count the number of paces that you take when venturing away from the main track (one large stride equals approxi-

CHECKLIST

Distance:	4 miles/6.4 km.
Ascent:	360ft/110m.
Approximate Time:	2 to 3 hours.
Maps:	1:25 000 OS Outdoor Leisure 5, The English Lakes, North Eastern area. 1:50 000 OS Landranger 90. 1:250 000 British Geological Survey 54N 04W, Lake District.
Terrain:	*WARNING – The lack of reference points on this flat open moorland can make route-finding difficult and this walk is not recommended in misty conditions.*
	It is also recommended that the appropriate OS map is used in conjunction with the route details described here and that both are studied carefully *before* setting out.
Degree of Shelter:	A low-level walk but with no natural shelter.
Stiles:	None.
Special Considerations:	All the Bronze Age sites visited are Scheduled Ancient Monuments. It is an offence to disturb or deface them or to use a metal detector within a 6.5ft/2m boundary of the archaeological feature.
Footwear:	On a dry day, trainers or walking shoes are adequate.
Parking:	There is room for up to 10 cars along the roadside at Roehead (NY479236).
Public Transport:	Buses connecting Penrith, Pooley Bridge and Patterdale (Stagecoach; service 108 every hour).

mately 3ft/1m) and relate this carefully to the positions of the sites on the map.

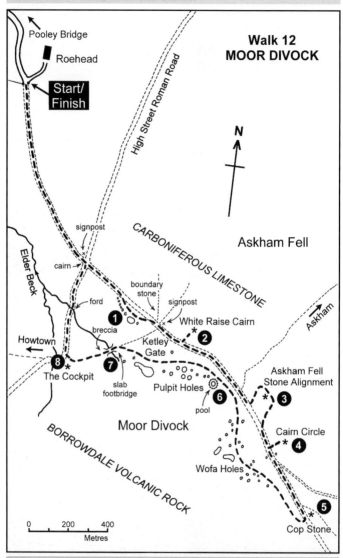

Walk 12
MOOR DIVOCK

Pooley Bridge

Roehead

Start/
Finish

N

High Street Roman Road

CARBONIFEROUS LIMESTONE

Askham Fell

signpost

cairn

Elder Beck

boundary
stone

signpost

White Raise Cairn

1

2

Askham

ford

breccia

Ketley
Gate

Howtown

8

The Cockpit

7

Pulpit Holes

slab
footbridge

pool

6

Askham Fell
Stone Alignment

3

Cairn Circle

4

Moor Divock

Wofa Holes

BORROWDALE VOLCANIC ROCK

5

Cop Stone

0   200   400
Metres

MOOR DIVOCK
SITE SUMMARY

1. **Line of shake-holes (NY486225)**
    Eight sunken holes in jointed limestone. Wild thyme and fairy flax.

2. **White Raise Cairn (NY489224)**
    Bronze Age burial chamber with stone 'cist'.

3. **Askham Fell Stone Alignment (NY493222)**
    22 stones in two parallel lines extending 230ft/70m in a north-west orientation.

4. **Ring Cairn (NY494220)**
    Circle of 10 large stones with central funeral cairn. Excavated finds include a Bronze Age vase.

5. **Cop Stone (NY496216)**
    A large standing stone is all that remains of a 65ft/20m diameter ring cairn. The circular earth bank can still be seen.

6. **Water-filled shake-hole (NY491223)**
    Breeding pool for dragonflies and damselflies.

7. **Peat deposits overlying volcanic rock (NY485224)**
    Fine example of brightly coloured breccia.

8. **The Cockpit (NY483223)**
    100ft/30m diameter stone circle containing 27 separate stones.

THE ROUTE

From Pooley Bridge take the road heading south-east past the church to the roundabout. Follow the sign to Hill Croft and continue on to **Roehead** where the road ends. Pass through the gate (sign: 'Barton Fell Common, No Cars or Motorcycles beyond this point') and follow the wide moorland track up a gentle gradient. At first there are few visible features except for a number of small grassy paths leading off through the bracken.

Continue straight ahead and notice how the track begins to divide the vegetation: bracken on the left, grass and heather on the right (bracken prefers to grow on dry ground and this is the key to understanding this area). At the top of this gently rising path, you eventually reach a cross-roads marked by a **signpost** and a large **cairn**. After approximately 650ft/200m begin looking amongst the grass and heather a few metres from the track on the right where you will see isolated rocks on the surface. They are the first features you meet in this flat landscape. The local bird population is aware of this and makes full use of them for perching and territorial display. Almost every stone you encounter from now on has a yellow top caused by lichen growing on the bird-droppings.

It is amongst these rocks that you will suddenly find your first shake-hole (**site 1**). Eight of them occupy a line parallel to the track and as you move along the line, they get wider and deeper. The seventh has a flat shelf with a patch of nettles before it drops down through layers of jointed limestone. In this sunken oasis there is wild thyme and fairy flax and in June and July you may catch site of a dragonfly. And that leaves a question: where is the water?

Rejoin the track and move on to the next junction. The block of stone less than 3ft/1m high is an old **boundary post** made of soft Penrith sandstone. It is covered in bird-droppings – but no lichen! Notice also how the wooden **signpost** nearby has been worn away and polished half a metre up from the ground. With so few places against which sheep can rub, when they do find something suitable, it gets well used.

About 500ft/150m past the signpost look for a group of stones above the bracken about 300ft/90m away from the track on your left. This is **White Raise Cairn** (**site 2**), a Bronze Age burial chamber that has been robbed. The central stone-lined compartment or 'cist' has had the lid removed and discarded alongside. The rock is white limestone. Notice the familiar yellow lichen where birds have perched and

The dragonfly pool at site 6

notice also the less-familiar patches of black as though the rocks have been splashed with tar. This is yet another lichen but this one grows specifically on limestone.

Retrace your steps back to the track. After 980ft/300m you pass a junction where a path to Askham leads off to the left. More stone monuments are hidden along this left side. In fact, as you walk in this southerly direction, all the Bronze Age sites except one are just to the left of the track and most of the shake-holes are on your right. You may also have noticed that most of the bracken is on your left with grass and heather to the right.

The key to these divisions lies with the geology and one explanation may involve the boundary lines of the underlying rock. From the moment you reached the first shake-hole, the road follows the edge of the carboniferous limestone that forms the north-east boundary of the Lake District. The bracken tells you what is underneath for it grows only on well-drained soil. As you move to the broken edge of the limestone, the underlying volcanic rocks begin to restrict the surface drainage. It is in this intermediate area where you find the shake-holes. Beyond this there are the usual volcanic rocks overlaid with peat.

After passing the Askham turn-off, and if the weather is clear, it is worthwhile exploring more carefully this left-hand side of the moor (**site 3**). The stones in this area are known as the **Askham Fell Stone Alignment** (National Monument number 22526). This is how they are described in the National Records:

> '*[The monument] is divided into two separate areas by a natural sink hole. The easterly part includes two virtually parallel align-ments of irregularly spaced stones 6m–9m apart, oriented approx-imately north-west – south-east, and running for a length of 70m. There are 15 stones in the northern line and seven stones in the southern line. Some of the stones remain upright while others appear to have fallen. The maximum height of the stones is 0.3m. At the south-east end there is a slight bank up to 0.1m high and 1m wide that continues the southernmost alignment of the stones for a further 8m. The western part of the monument continues approximately on the same alignment as the northern line of stones for a further 44m and includes seven irregularly spaced stones up to 0.45m high.*' (With permission, from The Secretary of State's Schedule Entry for Askham Fell Stone Alignment, SM 22526, 7th August 1995)

Such alignments are thought to have been associated with funeral ceremonies and other rituals and are dated at around the early part of the second millennium BC.

On returning back to the track, notice that the surface changes at a particular point. You are now walking on dry grass on top of a lime-stone pavement. After about 650ft/200m along from this point, look for a grassy path through the bracken on your left and follow it for approx-imately 330ft/100m. You eventually reach one of the most impressive Bronze Age monuments in the area: a **Ring Cairn** made of 10 large upright boulders (**site 4**).

Inside the ring of stones is a cairn of small stones with a hollow in the centre. An archaeological excavation of the site revealed an adult cremation with some pottery. One of the finds has been identified as a Yorkshire Vase and is now in the British Museum.

Before returning to the track, look for a patch of low heather a few metres to the south of the circle. Among the stems, try spotting a finely branched lichen that looks like a miniature wind-blown tree (its scien-

'In June and July you may catch site of a dragonfly – but where is the water?'

tific name, *Cladonia arbuscula*, is taken from the Latin word *arbor* meaning 'a tree'). This plant is in fact sold in model shops to make miniature trees for miniature railways!

On returning to the track the ground dips, producing an uncharacteristic muddy area before passing between two shake-holes. Keep straight ahead on the main track and after about 980ft/300m you will reach a large standing stone known as the **Cop Stone** (**site 5**). This was thought to have been part of a second ring cairn with a diameter of over 65ft/20m. There are records going back to the 1880s that recall a circle containing 10 large stones laid flat along a stone-filled bank. If you examine the ground north of the Cop Stone you can still see the remains of the circular bank but the recumbent stones are now missing.

This is the furthest point reached on the walk. From here the return journey takes you away from the main track to explore the opposite side. There is still no sign of the water that attracted the dragonfly seen earlier. The OS Outdoor Leisure map shows an elongated shake-hole with surface water (marked on the map as **Wofa Holes**) but the only suggestion of water that I was able to find in this area was a galvanised water tank that had been 'dumped' here!

The next possibility is marked on the map opposite the Askham turn-off. When you reach this junction (NY491222), look for a faint path leading to a fenced-off area about 330ft/100m up on the left. It is shown on the map as the first in a series of deep holes called the **Pulpit Holes** (**site 6**).

The wire fence looks promising, but it doesn't prepare you for what is ahead. Here is the dragonfly's water, in a deep **pool** crater filled to the brim, complete with island and young willow trees. Throughout this entire walk there have been no trees or standing water. Now that you have walked *uphill* from the track, you find them!

In the water there is yellow iris whilst around the edge there are tall clumps of soft rush. It is amongst the rushes that you will find the dragonflies. Look for the 'large red damselfly', darting out like sparks from a fire (its scientific name, *Pyrrhosoma*, comes from the Greek meaning 'fiery body'). Then there are the 'common blues' – the males of which are a striking electric-blue colour. If you are fortunate, you may see one of Britain's largest dragonflies – the 'gold-ringed hawker' with a wingspan of four inches. If it is dull or wet, they will not be flying but you may spot their larval nymphs hunting for beetles under the water.

It is easy to lose direction *en route* to the next site and if visibility is poor, a safe alternative is to return to the track and continue on to the junction of **Ketley Gate** (from here you can join the path leading to the next site by following the signpost left to Howtown). If the weather is clear, follow the line of shake-holes leading north-west across the moor until you reach the same path. Suddenly you have stepped off the limestone and onto volcanic rock overlaid with peat. The ground is water-logged and you find the first signs of flowing water at the start of **Elder Beck** (**site 7**).

Notice how the path along here has been made of stones raised above the peat and how the acids in the peat have bleached the rocks white. Immediately after crossing a small stone-slab footbridge, look for a large flat boulder on the right. Geologists call this rock '**breccia**'. It is made up of chunks of different rocks gathered from around the area and held together in a volcanic 'glue'. The mixture of colours is quite spectacular and is seen at its best when the surface is wet.

Continue over a boggy section fringed with rushes until you reach the grassy approach leading up to **The Cockpit** (**site 8**). This is the only monument on Moor Divock that has not been built on limestone. It is also the largest individual Bronze Age feature in the area with 27 stones

The Cop Stone – all that remains of a former stone circle

arranged in a 100ft/30m diameter circle. The path leading to it from the south-west is the High Street Roman road.

From The Cockpit head north along the continuation of the Roman road. For a brief moment you are on rocks from the Skiddaw Group that extend across from Ullswater. Cross the **ford** over Elder Beck and turn left at the large **cairn** to rejoin the moorland track back to your starting point at Roehead.

Walk 13

KNIPE SCAR

As you approach from Askham, you know you are entering some-where different when you have to get out of the car to open a gate on the public road; from the moment you hear the church bell at Bampton Grange chime the quarter.

You are still in the Lake District National Park but this area east of Haweswater is relatively unknown. Few visitors have heard of the place names – Whale and Howgate Foot – and yet this quiet limestone country has a long history of settlement dating back to the Bronze Age.

There are the remains of stone circles and medieval enclo-sures. There are 19th Century limekilns and a limestone pave-ment with all the wild flowers that you would expect plus the added interest of 'erratics' scattered over its surface.

This is a quiet place to come and get a feel for the past: a place to speculate on how things used to be.

THE ROUTE

From the road that crosses Knipe Moor, follow the wall leading up from the **cattle grid**. This section is sheltered from the south by a plantation of oak, ash and hawthorn. Continue following the wall to where the ground becomes level. In front there is a group of sycamores growing where the wall turns a corner (**site 1**). You are standing in a shallow depression that runs north-west along the base of Knipe Scar. A short distance from the wall on the left are two isolated stones resting on the finely grazed turf. They are quite different from the surrounding lime-stone. The largest is 1.5ft/0.5m high and has been polished smooth by the continuous rubbing of sheep. The smaller stone alongside is unpol-ished but of a similar material.

Geologists call these stones '**erratics**'. They have been picked up and carried by a moving glacier. They lie where they were dropped when the ice melted and their distribution reveals the path taken by

CHECKLIST

Distance:	2.1 miles/3.4km.
Ascent:	500ft/150m.
Approximate Time:	2 hours.
Maps:	1:25 000 OS Outdoor Leisure 5, The English Lakes, North Eastern area. 1:50 000 OS Landranger 90.
Terrain:	Gentle gradients over mostly dry grassland.
Degree of Shelter:	Fairly sheltered on the lower slopes of the scar. Exposed along the limestone pavement.
Stiles:	None.
Special Considerations:	The ring cairn on Knipe Scar is a Scheduled Ancient Monument. It is an offence to disturb or deface it or use a metal detector within 6.5ft/2m of its boundary.
Footwear:	In dry weather, walking shoes are quite adequate.
Parking:	There is ample parking space on the grass verge south of the cattle grid (NY522187).
Public Transport:	Limited bus service from Penrith to Bampton on certain days of the week (Stagecoach; service 111 and 957).

the ice-flow. These particular stones at site 1 are composed of Borrowdale Volcanic rock from the central Lake District. They are the first of many erratics that you will see on this walk.

Continue following the wall as it juts out around a curious corner. Look closely at the side of the wall and you will see that suddenly the stones change, becoming larger and carefully dressed. In fact this was once the side of an old building complete with a doorway! It has been incorporated into the wall and explains the rectangular bulge in the corner of this field enclosure. A study of old Ordnance Survey maps confirms this. The first edition OS map of this area printed in 1863 shows a building on this site. On the second edition, printed in 1899, the building has disappeared!

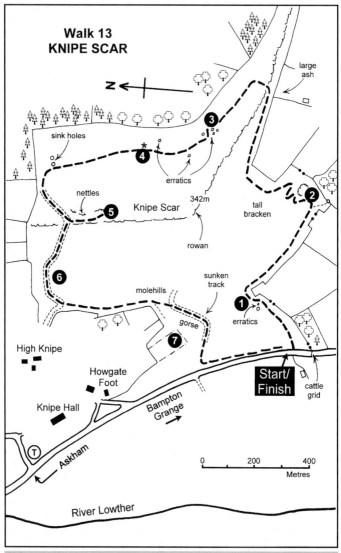

Walk 13
KNIPE SCAR

large ash

sink holes

erratics

nettles

Knipe Scar

342m

tall bracken

rowan

molehills

sunken track

gorse

erratics

High Knipe

Howgate Foot

Start/Finish

cattle grid

Knipe Hall

Bampton Grange

Askham

River Lowther

0   200   400
Metres

KNIPE SCAR
SITE SUMMARY

1. **Corner of field wall (NY523189)**
   Evidence of former building incorporated into
   stone wall. Volcanic erratics polished by sheep.

2. **Limekilns (NY527187)**
   Two kilns of different construction; the most recent
   has its firebrick lining exposed.

3. **Erratics (NY529191)**
   Different coloured rocks brought here by ice.
   Possibly associated with Bronze Age 'avenues'
   linking cairns and stone circles.

4. **Stone circle (NY529193)**
   50ft/15m diameter circular clearing with a
   limestone block at its centre.

5. **Quarried face (NY526194)**
   300 million year old fossil corals found in broken
   limestone fragments.

6. **Ridge and furrow (NY524196)**
   Evidence of ancient cultivation strips on a fertile
   shelf.

7. **Enclosure (NY521192)**
   Rectangular outline of buried walls suggests a long
   history of settlement along this shallow valley.

Follow the wall as it turns right. The path climbs gently and after
1300ft/400m turns left away from the wall up the slope between tall
bracken. In front of you there are two limekilns (**site 2**) that appear to

have been built at different times. The left-hand kiln is built on a square plan with a Romanesque arch typical of the early to mid-1800s. The right-hand kiln has lost most of its outer wall but the inside 'pot' can still be seen. It is lined with yellow firebrick indicating a later kiln, probably built after 1850. Look closely at the lining and how the silica-rich bricks have almost burnt away in the intense heat of the firing process. Temperatures inside these kilns would reach 1000 degrees C as the limestone was converted into quicklime. A draw-hole at the base was kept open to maintain a constant draft of air to remove the carbon dioxide.

The path at this point may vary depending on the time of year and whether the farmer has cleared a way through by cutting down the **tall bracken**. Keep parallel with the field walls on your right and once you have reached the top corner, follow the wall closely along a narrow sheep-track. You are walking about 16ft/5m away from the wall above a line of old hawthorns. All along this section there are thistles, some of which are only found growing on limestone. Look for carline thistle which is quite short with a large solitary straw-coloured head.

Continue along the sheep-track until you reach a **large ash**. Turn left and climb up the grassy slope to a gap in the limestone scar above. On a clear day there are fine views to the south-west to the High Street range. To the north-west, the more familiar outline of Blencathra can be seen on the skyline. But it is the foreground that holds the eye. This is a classic limestone pavement. There is no definite summit, just a wide promenade of clints and grykes with herb robert, wild thyme, eyebright, wall rue and thistles.

Why are there so many thistles on limestone? The high level of calcium in the soil is one factor. Such fertile land has traditionally been well grazed by sheep which leave thistles well alone whilst removing other competing plants. And perhaps the air currents created by the miniature corridors and canyons over the surface of the pavement encourage the settling of thistledown?

One of the characteristic features of the limestone pavements all across northern England is the large number of erratic boulders. There is evidence that many of them were used during the Bronze Age to construct avenues linking cairns and stone circles. Three ceremonial avenues were thought to have been built around Shap and one of these was believed to have extended north in a single row of stones across Knipe Scar. Today only a few isolated stones from these avenues survive

The quarry cave and pool at site 2, Rydal (Walk 17) (© Heather Lyon)

The oak tree with the strange growth at site 2, Stock Ghyll Force (Walk 18)

Platform at site 5 where diatomite was brought ashore, Kentmere (Walk 19)

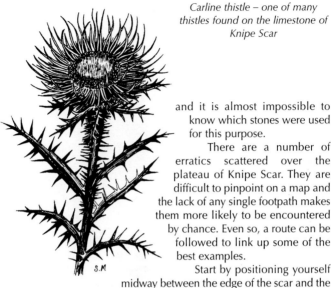

Carline thistle – one of many thistles found on the limestone of Knipe Scar

s.M

and it is almost impossible to know which stones were used for this purpose.

There are a number of erratics scattered over the plateau of Knipe Scar. They are difficult to pinpoint on a map and the lack of any single footpath makes them more likely to be encountered by chance. Even so, a route can be followed to link up some of the best examples.

Start by positioning yourself midway between the edge of the scar and the wall that runs along the north-east side and follow a route parallel with and approximately 330ft/100m from the wall. This should bring you to your first erratic at **site 3**. Here is a cluster of three stones, the largest of which is topped with yellow lichen (the birds choose only the highest points for their look-outs). Other **erratics** can be found further ahead, all of which show the same lichen pattern.

If you continue parallel with the wall keeping a distance of about 160–200ft/50–60m, you should eventually find a wooden post in a small clearing in the bracken (**site 4**). This marks the site of what was once described as a 'Druids' Circle' but is now officially designated as a Ring Cairn. It is very difficult amongst the bracken to find much evidence of this Bronze Age feature. The description from the Cumbria Sites and Monuments Record may help:

'An area of broken limestone pavement, some of which appears to have been cleared, the slabs being arranged to form a circle. Smaller stones projecting from the turf between these slabs give the perimeter the appearance of a low bank. In the centre of the

circle, which has an internal diam of approx 15m, there is a lime-stone block. Other blocks are scattered in the SW and NW quadrants.' (With permission, T Clare; MA thesis)

Continue across the limestone pavement until you almost reach the wall forming the northern boundary of the scar. Here are two circular depressions in the grass. They are shallow **sink holes** often found on limestone where the subsurface has either collapsed or been slowly dissolved.

From the sink holes, head west along the line of the wall until you reach a broad, grassy track that takes you across some exposed pavement and down along to the edge of the scar. Leave the track and follow the edge of the scar for approximately 400ft/120m to reach **site 5**.

Here is a quarried face with a small sycamore and a hawthorn growing out from the top. Scattered along the foot of the rock face are pieces of limestone, some of which contain fossil corals that lived 300 million years ago in warm shallow seas just north of the equator.

Retrace your steps along the edge of the scar back to the broad, grassy track. Follow this down to a level area covered in thistles. You are now at **site 6**, an extensive area of 'ridge and furrow' marks. This type of cultivation is difficult to date but is likely to have started here in the medieval period (11th–16th Century).

The track continues down to High Knipe Farm. Do not take this route but instead turn off left above the field walls and follow the muddy sheep-tracks. Eventually you join a sunken path that leads down between some tall **gorse** bushes.

The ground in front drops gently into a shallow, grassy valley before reaching the road. If the sun is low, you will see the grassed-over walls of an ancient enclosure (**site 7**). It is difficult to know the age of these walls. Some may be contemporaneous with the Bronze Age features high up on Knipe Scar although they are more likely to be linked with the ridge and furrow markings at site 6. They are certainly much older than the present farm buildings and stone walls which cut straight through them. Follow the road back to your start point.

Walk 14

MARTINDALE

*By Lakeland standards, few people visit Martindale. There is no
through-road and the surrounding hills are not at the top of the
fellwalker's list. Those who do venture this far may visit the Old
Church and then return to Howtown to catch the Ullswater
'Steamer' or continue back along the narrow road to Pooley
Bridge. This has left an area relatively unexplored close to one of
Lakeland's busiest centres.*

*The walk described here is one of the shortest in the book
but it highlights a recurring theme of looking at the landscape at
close quarters. Martindale is not the place for a route-march. It
is a place to slow down and take in the detail – to enjoy those
things that are often overlooked in the rush to cover distance.*

*There is a saying: avoid leaving anything behind except your
footprints. Well, on this walk, such is its delicate character, there
are places where even the footprints are a problem! There is,
however, something satisfying in venturing onto 'untouched'
ground; in looking without disturbing. For a brief moment you
become an explorer, walking into a Lakeland that is virtually
unknown.*

The Route

The focal point of this quiet dale is the **Old Church** of Saint Martin and
this is where our walk begins (**site 1**).

The building in front of you has been here for over 400 years but if
you look along the base of the south wall you will see the foundation
of a much older chapel built over 700 years ago. But even this impressive history is predated by a far older occupant of the site – 'The
Martindale Yew'.

This female tree at the north-east corner of the church has a girth
of 19ft/5.8m and is believed to be 1500 years old ('believed to be'

because once a yew gets beyond 1000 years it is difficult to date accurately as the inside becomes hollow leaving no continuous tree-ring record). From Celtic times, the yew has been regarded as a sacred tree and its position here would have influenced the building of the first church on this site.

As you stand underneath its massive branches, look for fragments of black feathers and wings on the ground between the wall and the stone tomb. Most years there is a dead rook here – often a young bird that has fallen from one

The cave-dwelling wren

of the nests above. The carcass decays very slowly because of the sterile conditions produced by the yew's toxins. This is why (coupled with the lack of sunlight) there is so little plantlife growing on and underneath its branches. No lichens grow here – only a fine green alga that is able to tolerate the tree's chemical defences.

It was therefore surprising that in the summer of 2000, an elderberry bush was found to have lodged itself and taken root in the crown of the tree. But such is the protection given to this grand old lady – the intruder was spotted and is to be removed with a chain-saw!

The first recorded curate of the church was Richard Birkett. It is fitting that it is his tomb that takes pride of place under this old yew. He was quite a character and took great care in the upkeep of the churchyard. A visitor to the church in 1688 refers to the '*neat*

CHECKLIST

Distance:	1.6 miles/2.6km.
Ascent:	560ft/170m.
Approximate Time:	1 hour.
Maps:	1:25 000 OS Outdoor Leisure 5, The English Lakes, North Eastern area. 1:50 000 OS Landranger 90.
Terrain:	Gently rising quarry path. Mostly dry and without difficulties.
Degree of Shelter:	The cave and church provide shelter from rain. The low-level path is sheltered from strong winds.
Stiles:	None.
Special Considerations:	Much of the charm of this walk is in discovering a path that is unspoilt and forgotten. Please take care to leave the area as you found it for others to enjoy particularly when visiting the cave.
	Optional extras that you may wish to take include a hand-lens and binoculars.
Footwear:	Boots (or walking shoes in dry weather).
Parking:	There is ample parking space in front of Martindale Old Church (NY434184).
Public Transport:	Stagecoach; service 517 (Bowness to Glenridding) and service 108 (Penrith to Patterdale) connect with the Ullswater 'Steamers'. Sailings are from Glenridding and Pooley Bridge to Howtown (telephone 017684 82229 for timetable). The walking distance from Howtown Pier to the Old Church is 1.3 miles/2.1km.

Chapelyard which by the peculiar care and industry of an old yeoman Sir Richard the Reader [Reverend Birkett] is kept clean and neat as a Bowling Green. In which particular he is so very extreamly curiouse that he will not suffer a mole to cast in it but setting all other occasions

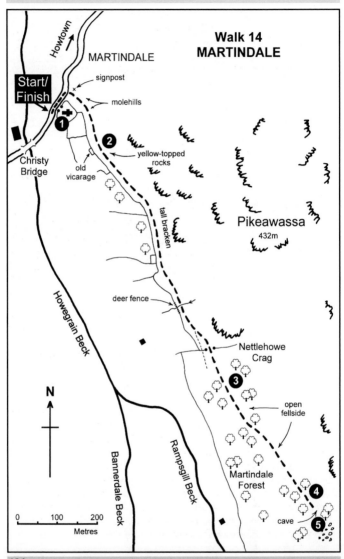

Walk 14
MARTINDALE

Howtown

MARTINDALE

Start/
Finish

signpost

molehills

1

2

yellow-topped
rocks

Christy
Bridge

old
vicarage

tall bracken

Pikeawassa

432m

deer fence

Howegrain Beck

Nettlehowe
Crag

3

open
fellside

N

0   100   200
Metres

Bannerdale Beck

Rampsgill Beck

Martindale
Forest

4

cave

5

MARTINDALE
SITE SUMMARY

1. **Church of St Martin (NY434184)**
   Famous 1500-year-old yew in north-east corner of
   churchyard. Sandstone pillar from High Street
   Roman road used as a baptismal font.

2. **Yellow-topped rocks (NY435183)**
   Lookout perches for local birdlife showing effects
   on lichen distribution.

3. **Engineered path (NY439177)**
   Path built on low wall to even out gradient for
   packhorses. On open fellside the path is hidden
   because of 'soil creep'.

4. **Dead ash trees (NY441175)**
   Standing and fallen dead trees covered in burrs
   resulting from insect attack.

5. **Quarry cave (NY441174)**
   Secluded setting. Damp floor covered in liverwort
   with leaves curling up towards the light.

*aside he will watch and kill her with his own hand and if his cow (which
doth sometimes graze there) leave any unseamly thing behind her, he
will take care to remove it himselfe with all possible diligence'* (from
The Martindale Registers, 1633–1890).

Before entering the church, take time to study the north wall.
Starting at the north-east corner, an old blocked-off doorway can be
seen alongside the second window. Further along to the right is a stone
carved with the date 1714. This is thought to commemorate the year
when many improvements were made including the addition of a flag-
stone floor and a porch on the west side.

Once inside the church, notice the small pillar of Penrith sandstone to the left of the altar. It was brought down from the Roman road on High Street where it was thought to have been a wayside shrine for the Roman soldiers. It was used by the local dalesfolk as a sharpening stone and the vertical scratch-marks made by the farm tools and knives can still be seen. Eventually it was taken inside the church and the hollowed-out top supported a basin which was used for baptisms.

After leaving the church and churchyard head north to join the path (**signpost**: 'Public Footpath') that takes you along the north side of the valley. The soil in this area is very fertile. If you look on the north-east side of the path you will often find **molehills** below the bracken indicating high calcium levels and a large population of earthworms. As you pass by the yew tree again, under the shelter of its branches, notice the chickweed amongst the grass. This is an opportunist weed whose fast growth enables it to spread where the grass has been suppressed.

The path follows the old wall and after about 330ft/100m passes the ruins of the original **vicarage** on the right. From here onwards you will find many small boulders bordering the path (**site 2**). The familiar **yellow-topped rocks** are the result of lichens growing on the nitrogen from bird-droppings. For this lichen to grow, a particular rock has to be used regularly by birds as a lookout perch.

Continue following the wall past a line of mature ash trees. The steep fellside on your left is covered in **tall bracken** which indicates the degree of shelter on this side of the valley. Above is the jagged skyline of Pikeawassa.

After crossing a small stream, the path splits. Take the left branch that leads through a gate in the wall. The path now becomes narrower and climbs gently up through the bracken. A quick glance at the Ordnance Survey map shows that you have entered Martindale Forest.

You pass three old hazel trees on the right and then a hawthorn before reaching a group of hazel, sycamore and bird cherry. The path along this section is built up as though on a low wall (**site 3**) making the gradient even and regular. This is the first indication that this is no casual walker's path but a route carefully constructed for packhorses. But where is it leading?

On the right of the path, try spotting a patch of 'aerial' wood sorrel that has taken root on the mossy trunk of an old hazel tree. A few metres further on, the path leads between two large oak trees. The left-hand tree has a large purple-red stone wedged under its exposed roots.

This is volcanic *tuff* or ash coloured with iron.

The path now becomes narrower as it climbs across an open area. Beyond the clearing you pass a group of hazel and then a large oak on the left. On its moss-covered trunk, notice a striking pale-green rectangular patch. Something has scraped the bark clean and the first plant to colonise the bare surface has been a fast-growing green alga.

The path narrows once again as you cross another area of **open fell-side**. You may have noticed that each time the path crosses open ground without the shelter of trees, it becomes less distinct. On angles of slope approaching 45 degrees the soil 'creeps' downwards and tends to hide

Wood sorrel amongst the trees of Martindale Forest

the path. In the wooded sections, the tree roots and the overhead shelter stabilise the soil and the path is not so disrupted.

If the weather is clear there are good views over your left shoulder to the spiky ridge of Pikeawassa before the path makes its way between more scattered hazels and hawthorns. In front of you is a patch of dead trees (**site 4**). These are the remains of old ash trees that have been attacked by various insects. The trees have been killed but they put up quite a battle in their struggle to isolate the attacking intruders. The result is an amazing scene of fallen trunks each one covered in a grotesque pattern of intricate 'burrs'. The rotting wood that remains now supports a raised garden of mosses and wild geraniums.

Once again the path can be seen to have been built on top of a low wall so as to ease the gradient and the reason lies just ahead. After a few steps you find yourself standing on the spoil-heap of the Martindale stone quarry (**site 5**). On the Ordnance Survey 1:25 000 map the quarry is marked as a '**cave**'. As you face the entrance, notice the drill-holes on each side where the charges were set for blasting. There are wrens nesting here (the scientific name for the wren is *Troglodytes troglodytes* which means 'the cave dweller').

Look inside the entrance. You feel as though you ought to remove your boots before entering! The floor is carpeted with the delicate green leaves of the liverwort, *Conocephalum*. Take a closer look at the top surface of this liverwort, preferably with a hand-lens or by looking through a reversed pair of binoculars. The pattern is caused by air chambers that are compressed into hexagons, each having a large central pore. Another characteristic is the plant's strange antiseptic smell. Normally these plants would grow flat against the rock. But here the forked branches curl up towards the light from the cave entrance. Like flat cartoon characters raising their heads, they could almost be looking back at you as you peer in at them!

The cave marks the furthest point of the walk. Progress beyond here is difficult as the path fades into sheep-tracks. From the cave, therefore, retrace your steps back to the starting point at the Old Church.

Silver Point – the view along the quarry path leading back to Patterdale

Walk 15

SILVER POINT

One of the most popular outings in the Patterdale area is the walk along Ullswater's southern shore from Side Farm to Howtown making the return journey to Glenridding by 'Steamer'. The shoreline walk, or 'Steamer-link path', is regarded by many as one of the finest in the district.

This particular route goes only as far as Silver Point and returns to Side Farm along the higher bridleway. I first did this walk in June when the lower shoreline path was busy with visitors making the link with the steamer. As soon as I turned off at Silver Point to follow the higher path, I met only one other person – a local lady from Patterdale walking her dog.

This is the perfect circular route from Patterdale if the weather turns foul and you need to get out for a few hours and stretch your legs. The hidden valley between Birk Fell and Silver Crag will be completely new to most people, and its variety of wild flowers is an unexpected delight.

THE ROUTE

From **Side Farm** follow the farm road heading north along the eastern shore of Ullswater. You pass through patches of mixed woodland keeping the stone wall on your left. The way is dark in places due to the thick canopy of mature beech and sycamore and, because of the shade, the wall has a thick covering of moss. Look for two yew trees growing behind the wall just before you get your first view of the lake (**site 1**). There is no moss growing on the wall underneath their branches, only a uniform covering of green algae that is usually only found in cities. The area below the yew is 'poisoned' by chemicals made by the tree. The green algae are all that can survive.

After passing a clearing with views across the lake, continue on past the **camp site**. The farm building up ahead on the left has a slate roof and its north-facing side is completely overgrown with moss under the shade of an ash. Notice the large number of nettles and foxgloves along this section of farm road – this is a regular feeding station for cattle, and the ground is frequently manured and trampled. This is also a good place to spot chaffinches and wagtails searching for left-over food.

Where the path forks right, keep straight ahead. After crossing a shallow stream you pass a gate on the left that has a sign which reads: 'CAUTION – THESE COWS MAY BE DANGEROUS'… Just pray that you don't meet the bull!

From now on the path gets narrower with views of open fellside on your right and mature parkland on your left. Eventually the path leads through tall bracken with extensive views of the lake. The wall that you have been following drops down towards the shore on the left whilst the path goes over a rocky outcrop.

You are now standing on a basalt dyke (**site 2**): a vertical band of once-liquid rock that squeezed its way through the solid surroundings. It is red and purple in places because it contains various forms of iron, and it crumbles because it was chilled from being liquid to solid very quickly. The resulting fertile soil supports a fine group of mature Scots pine.

Continue through the **tall bracken** with patches of juniper and holly on each side. At **Silver Point** bear right over a narrow stream and after a further 330ft/100m take a narrow turn-off to the right marked by a small **cairn**.

You leave the busy 'steamer-link path' and begin to climb what feels like your own private valley. The path makes its way through a juniper grove along a delightful section that has been constructed over a stone terrace (**site 3**). There is scree down on your right and steep crags above. The wild flowers in between are exquisite – herb robert, wild thyme, lady's-mantle and wild strawberries. On the loose scree you will find parsley fern. The path then begins to level out as you follow the line of a low wall. Cross the wall and follow the path over a wide grassy level area.

On your left there is a small tarn (**site 4**). There are things here you won't have seen before. Look below the surface in May or June and there will be dragonfly nymphs hunting their prey. Look closer and you will see tadpoles hiding under the delicate floating water-plants. Further along, the path rises to a wide grassy col. Notice the small rock in front. It is covered in bird-lime that is tinged purple – a result of the local bird population eating **juniper** berries. Some places stay in the

CHECKLIST

Distance:	3 miles/4.7km.
Ascent:	330ft/100m.
Approximate Time:	2 to 3 hours.
Maps:	1:25 000 OS Outdoor Leisure 5, The English Lakes, North Eastern area. 1:50 000 OS Landranger 90.
Terrain:	Easy, level path as far as Silver Point. The higher return path is more rugged but well defined.
Degree of Shelter:	A low-level walk, mostly sheltered from the wind.
Stiles:	None.
Special Considerations:	Please do not pick the wild flowers. If you need a record, take a photograph.
Footwear:	Boots.
Parking:	Side Farm (NY398163) provides parking for a small fee.
Public Transport:	Stagecoach buses to Patterdale; service 491 from Ambleside (summer service), service 108 from Penrith at least every 2 hours at least six days a week.

memory and this secret valley is one of them.

You now descend a broad grassy path. Notice the bell heather (*Erica cinerea*) covering the crag up on your right. Where the path levels out, look for a prominent **boulder** just off to the right before the bracken begins. There is the usual mustard-coloured lichen covering the top (because of the bird-droppings) but this is also a good place for spotting 'crottle' – a grey, leafy lichen that was used for dying wool. It is one of the few plant dyes that doesn't require a mordant. It provides the brown and gold colours of Harris Tweed.

The path now follows a pleasant terraced track that was constructed for the use of quarry ponies. The surface has patches of dark-**red basalt** rock where it cuts through the basalt dyke (the same dyke that you saw

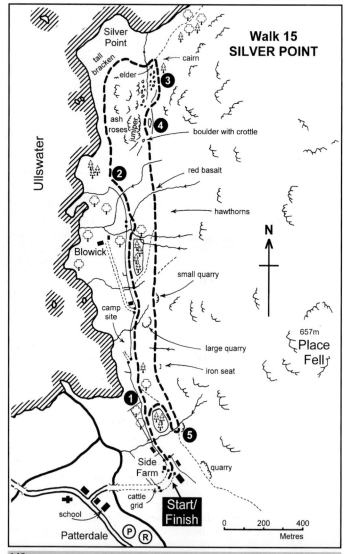

**Walk 15
SILVER POINT**

Silver
Point

tall bracken

← cairn

elder

3

ash
roses

4

← boulder with crottle

Ullswater

2

red basalt

← hawthorns

N

Blowick

small quarry

camp
site

large quarry

657m
**Place
Fell**

iron seat

1

5

quarry

Side
Farm

cattle
grid

**Start/
Finish**

school

Patterdale (P) (R)

0   200   400
Metres

SILVER POINT
SITE SUMMARY

1. **Yew trees (NY397166)**
   Effect of poisons produced by trees on plantlife growing on wall below.

2. **Basalt dyke (NY395177)**
   An intrusion of fertile volcanic rock containing iron (stained purple and red) and supporting fine growths of mature Scots pine.

3. **Juniper grove (NY398182)**
   Natural juniper woodland with field layer of alpine flowers including lady's-mantle and wild strawberry.

4. **Valley head (NY397179)**
   Secluded tarn with dragonflies and frogs.

5. **Quarry entrance (NY398165)**
   Water-curtain and miniature gill with rich variety of wild flowers and ferns.

on the lower path). After crossing a stream, the track drops and becomes more stony. You cross a line of **hawthorns** and then two more streams (avoiding the path down to your right).

You are now approaching an area of fellside that was extensively quarried for building-stone. Keep a look out for spoil-heaps that mark the entrances. The first one you pass is a **small quarry** on the left alongside an ash tree. A few metres further there is a tooth-shaped boulder that indicates the position of a much larger cavern hidden down on the right, below two spreading ash trees.

Further along the path there is a Victorian wrought-**iron seat**. This

The Victorian wrought-iron seat on the return path above Ullswater

is not unusual in the Lake District (they have even been found on some of the fell tops). What makes this different is the quality of the iron. This is bare metal and yet it shows hardly any corrosion. Incorporated in the design of the backrest is the date: 18VR97.

Beyond the seat the path drops down over a rough stony section which leads to a narrow quarry on the left (**site 5**). Just before you reach the opening, notice how the water coming down the fellside stops at the path and turns back to disappear underground. Water also pours over the cave entrance. The quarrying has created a miniature gill and waterfall with a surprising variety of wild flowers and ferns. There is ash, hazel and wild rose. Even the spoil-heap is covered in wild thyme.

Follow the path as it swings sharp right to bring you underneath the pile of spoil. The strange noise coming from below ground is the water that disappeared into the cave above. It finally emerges to cross the path at the foot of the spoil. Continue along the path until you reach the corner of a walled enclosure where you can drop down left to join the farm road back to Side Farm.

Walk 16

FOUR STONES HILL

Visitors to Haweswater tend to head up the valley to climb the High Street ridges, or walk across to Riggindale to see the golden eagles and the exposed walls of Mardale village. Those walking the north-west shore of the reservoir have their sights set on Robin Hood's Bay. Why else should anyone visit Haweswater?

The path to Four Stones Hill, an ancient Bronze Age site complete with standing stones, ancient cairns and 'dew pond', is virtually unknown. The cascading waterfalls, old copper workings and peregrines are passed by. At any point on this walk, you are less than 2 miles/3km from the Haweswater Dam and yet there is enough here to occupy the keenest archaeologist and birdwatcher for the full day.

This is a walk for those who have 'done' the Lake District and think there is little fresh to discover. When the last 'Wainwright' has been completed, a visit to Four Stones Hill is recommended to show just how much there is still left to see.

THE ROUTE

From **Burnbanks** follow the signs: 'Public Footpath fellside track via NW shore of Haweswater'. The path takes you past the labourers' cottages under a dark canopy of sycamore and eventually brings you out through a gate with the open fell on your right. (*Please note that the Public Right of Way along this section has been incorrectly marked on current OS maps.*) On your left is a thin band of woodland which hides your view of the reservoir until you reach the Heltondale Beck **tunnel** (marked by a slate plaque set in the stone wall). The path continues with intermittent breaks in the trees to your left. Most of these trees were planted after the dam was built and they comprise a strange mixture of evergreens and deciduous including some copper beech. Not until you meet the first bit of original Mardale wall do you find the original Mardale trees (**site 1**). Here on the right of the path are the more familiar holly, rowan and ash growing together.

As you approach the foot of **Measand Beck** you begin to hear the waterfalls. Cross the wooden footbridge and notice the scent of wood sage (especially if it's raining) that grows by the line of iron posts. Leave the reservoir track and take the narrow path that keeps closely to the left side of the beck. It is steep and rocky in places with intermittent views of the cascading waterfalls. You are walking over hard volcanic rock that intruded into the surrounding lavas. Eventually, you reach the edge of this 'fertile' intrusion where the path widens and becomes grassy as it levels out. Below you on the right is a sunken dell where the beck flows gently around a grassy island surrounded by wild rose, honeysuckle, birch and willow before rushing through a narrow gorge lined with bell heather. This fertile area marking the edge of the intrusion extends over a broad, grassy area to the left of the path (**site 2**). Notice the molehills. Wherever you have outcrops of fertile, basic non-acidic rock with high calcium levels you will have earthworms, and moles eat earthworms.

A little further along and about 50ft/15m off to the left there is a large isolated boulder. There are all sorts of things going on here. This is a favourite perch for kestrels. Look for traces of food-pellets on the top. Notice also how the lichens grow in circular zones like concentric bands around a dartboard. Around the outside is dark brown; inside is light grey whilst around the 'bull's-eye' is mustard-yellow, showing the different concentrations of nitrogen as you approach the centre.

If it's wet you should also see grey slugs feeding on the surface. Grey slugs have a residual shell hidden under the skin and need calcium in their diet. They are found (along with snails) where there are basic rocks. Elsewhere on boggy upland sites, where there is a shortage of calcium, you will find only the large black slug (*Arion ater*) – one of the few slugs that doesn't have a residual shell.

Continue on the level, grassy path to the wooden footbridge (**site 3**). Look for dippers flying underneath. You may also hear stonechats calling from the surrounding bracken. After crossing the bridge there are a number of narrow tracks that fan out in front of you. Choose the one that leads directly ahead as you leave the bridge. This is the path to Four Stones Hill. It is rarely used and has become indistinct in places amongst the encroaching bracken. It keeps to a fairly even gradient in a north-east direction and eventually brings you within sight of the two standing stones towards which you are heading.

This whole area was once settled during the Bronze Age and the

CHECKLIST

Distance:	4.2 miles/6.7km
Ascent:	670ft/205m.
Approximate Time:	3 to 4 hours.
Maps:	1:25 000 OS Outdoor Leisure 5, The English Lakes, North Eastern area. 1:50 000 OS Landranger 90. 1: 250 000 British Geological Survey 54N 04W, Lake District.
Terrain:	Broad, level track alongside reservoir followed by a short, rocky climb. The moorland section is mostly dry and grassy but the path is ill-defined in places.
Degree of Shelter:	Good shelter along the tree-lined sections of the reservoir track.
Stiles:	None.
Special Considerations:	*In misty conditions, this walk should only be attempted by walkers who are experienced at route-finding using a map and compass.*
	The Bronze Age sites in this area are all Scheduled Ancient Monuments. It is an offence to disturb or deface them or use a metal detector within a 6.5ft/2m boundary of the feature. The mine shafts at site 5 are flooded and dangerous and should not be approached.
Footwear:	Boots.
Parking:	There is space at Burnbanks at the road junction (NY508161).
	Please do not block the garage entrances opposite the cottages further along.
Public Transport:	A limited bus service from Penrith to Burnbanks (Stagecoach; services 111 and 957, one bus per day on certain days of the week).

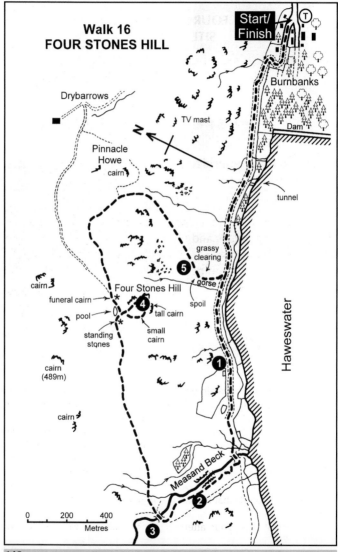

Walk 16
FOUR STONES HILL

Start/Finish

Burnbanks

Drybarrows

TV mast

N

Pinnacle Howe
cairn

Dam

tunnel

grassy clearing

5

gorse

cairn

Four Stones Hill

funeral cairn

spoil

pool

4

tall cairn

standing stones

small cairn

cairn
(489m)

1

cairn

Haweswater

Measand Beck

2

0   200   400
Metres

3

FOUR STONES HILL
SITE SUMMARY

1. **Mardale trees (NY491157)**
    Original village wall with local deciduous trees.

2. **Fertile grassy shelf (NY484156)**
    Kestrel feeding-perch. Molehills and grey slugs
    indicate soil calcium levels.

3. **Wooden footbridge (NY483157)**
    Dippers flying under bridge and stonechats in
    surrounding bracken.

4. **Four Stones Hill summit (NY492163)**
    Feeding ledges and soaring slopes for peregrines
    and golden eagles. Views down onto Bronze Age
    cairns and standing stones.

5. **Haweswater copper mines (NY494161)**
    Three separate levels (Caution! Deep shafts).
    Samples of brightly coloured copper ore found on
    spoil-heaps.

geology may help to explain why. The same fertile, basic rock that you
passed on your way up forms all the high ground that you see in front.
From Four Stones Hill and across onto the opposite ridge of this hidden
valley, you are enclosed within a horseshoe of volcanic dykes. Within
this one square kilometre, there are 18 listed archaeological sites dating
back to the Bronze and Iron Age periods. This was likely to have been
a highly successful upland settlement on fertile land during a period of
good weather. An analysis of pollen found in the sediments of
Haweswater suggests that the climate at that time was much drier than
the present day.

In front of you, your attention is inevitably drawn to the two

standing stones. The name Four Stones Hill suggests that there should be another two, and a second pair was described in a 1901 publication, *History of the Parish of Bampton* by M E Noble. Here is her description of the scene:

> '…two menhirs or standing stones, looking like forgotten gateposts of the roughest description. They are about 4ft/1.2m high, and not set in the ground. Consequently the frequent rubbing of sheep has worn away the ground, and they are now much out of the perpendicular. Two similar stones not far away seem to have fallen from this cause.'

Unfortunately, further surveys since this description was made have been unable to locate the second pair.

The next feature that you pass is the **pool** of water occupying an eliptical hollow to the left of the path. This dries up in the course of a normal summer and if the climate was dry during the Bronze Age, it must have been an unreliable source. Look carefully around the perimeter and you will see a line of rocks that have been carefully arranged suggesting that this was deliberately constructed to act as a 'dew pond' to increase the amount of usable water on this dry upland site.

From the pond, leave the path and climb the rough fellside to the top of **Four Stones Hill**. Make your way to the south-east edge overlooking the reservoir (**site 4**). To appreciate the full significance of this spot, you need to stand here in June with a south-east wind blowing. You will then hear the peregrines: two adults and as many as three young in most years. This is not their nest site, but with the wind in this direction this is their favourite slope for soaring and catching prey. Look at the ledge in front. The grass here is a darker shade of green and is littered with food-pellets and the remains of small birds. The last time I was here there were a number of pellets measuring up to three inches long that could only have come from the golden eagles nesting further up the valley. This is a place to stay a while and let the wildlife come to you.

A few hundred metres below, there is a beautifully constructed **tall cairn** on a prominent rock platform (the cairn on Lingmell used to look like this). The skyline in this area is dotted with various cairns, some of which are modern whilst others belong to the same period as the standing stones. If you head west, you drop down to a **small cairn** that lines up with a cairn on the opposite skyline directly in line with the two standing stones. But it is difficult to assess the significance of such alignments without knowing the dates of the cairns involved. As you walk back towards the standing stones keep a look-out for the remains of a stone shelter built out from the crags on your right. It looks quite old and undisturbed.

Continue past the **pool** until you reach a large pile of stones – thought to be a **funeral cairn**. Once again there is the problem of finding modern artefacts associated with those that are prehistoric. In this case, the original Bronze Age cairn has been recently disturbed in the centre and some of the stones have been used to form a circular shelter.

From the cairn, two tracks lead off in front of you. Take the fainter right-hand path that drops down between bracken. After crossing a boggy patch with a small stream, you pass through a grassy area leading to a damp hollow with rushes. The path follows the stony water-course (dried up in places) and then crosses it, bearing right along a well-marked path that skirts along the edge of a large area of bracken.

This path leads across a wet hollow full of rushes and climbs up to the saddle in the crags facing you. Don't follow this. Instead, when you reach the wet hollow, bear off to the right following the line of the gently sloping water-course. The path is indistinct along this section but aim for a gentle descent along to your right until you reach a grassed-over elongated mound. This is the first of three copper mines along this side of Four Stones Hill (**site 5**).

You eventually reach a **grassy clearing** in the bracken. Just up to the right through a clump of **gorse** bushes there is a large area of spoil. Some of the rocks still show traces of the rich copper ore and take on striking refractory colours from orange to purple. One of the shafts is over 55ft/17m deep. It is extremely dangerous and should not be entered. Return to the grassy clearing and drop down to join the shore-line path which will take you back to Burnbanks.

Walk 17

RYDAL

Over 200 years ago, Rydal Cave was not a place for holiday-makers to visit. It was a busy working quarry with its own road system for supplying the surrounding villages with building stone. Nowadays, the industry is tourism and the cave is a major attraction. The pool of water at its entrance, once choked with stone slurry, is now crystal-clear and full of fish. The spoil-heaps are colonised by rock plants, and the quarry road is a favourite tree-lined path.

This is a short, gentle walk suitable for all age groups. The young will find plenty of places to explore and the elders can tell of plants that eat insects and some that break bones! And if the heavens should open, you will be guaranteed a lunchbreak with a dry roof over your head!

THE ROUTE

From **White Moss** Common car park head west along the footpath that leads towards the **ford** and footbridge. Before reaching the bridge, keep a look-out on the left of the path for birch trees infected with the razor-strop fungus (once used as an alternative to leather for sharpening razors). In this low-lying area alongside the water, the air is often still and damp – ideal conditions for this bracket fungus which invariably kills birch trees.

Once over the next footbridge, follow the path that takes you across the river connecting Rydal Water with Grasmere. You have now entered a mature broad-leaved woodland. Approximately 820ft/250m past the bridge on the right you pass a **large beech** with its network of roots raised above the bare soil. Notice how dark it has become. This is typical of beech with its dense foliage and the result is that very little plantlife can grow beneath it except moss. Without the stabilising effect of grass, the soil quickly erodes away exposing the tree's roots.

The path now starts to climb and goes over a smooth lump of **rock**

CHECKLIST

Distance:	2.7 miles/4.3km.
Ascent:	200ft/60m.
Approximate Time:	2 hours.
Maps:	1:25 000 OS Outdoor Leisure 7, The English Lakes, South Eastern area.
Terrain:	Dry footpaths. Mostly level or gentle gradients.
Degree of Shelter:	Very sheltered throughout the entire walk. It may be too sheltered if there are midges about!
Stiles:	None.
Special Considerations:	Suitable for all ages and capabilities.
Footwear:	Walking shoes or boots.
Parking:	Ample parking space at White Moss Common (NY351065).
Public Transport:	Buses from Ambleside (Stagecoach; services 555 and 559 every hour most days).

that has been polished by the action of an ice sheet. After skirting around a miniature valley with a small stream running alongside a wall, the path makes its way through the dense woodland until it reaches a gate leading out onto the open fell. A broad path follows the wall. Do not take this route. Instead, climb a narrow path that leads up the slope directly ahead through tall bracken.

After crossing a stream, look for the junction of another path joining in on the right. At this point you should see a large, isolated boulder about 65ft/20m to the left (**site 1**). This can be reached by taking a narrow path through the bracken. Once again you see the polished surface caused by ice. The area surrounding Rydal Water is composed mostly of boulder clay carried here during the last Ice Age and this is one of the volcanic rocks that was dropped here when the ice melted. Take a close look at its west-facing side. There is a line of drill-holes used for setting explosive charges – evidence that it was once split for

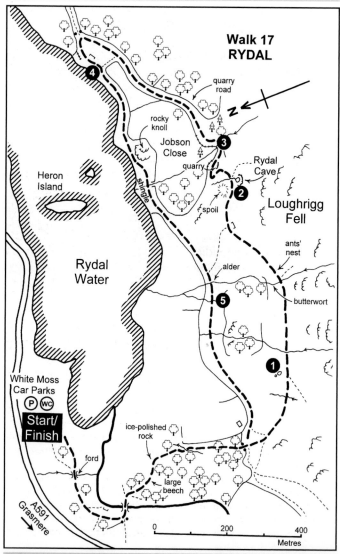

**Walk 17
RYDAL**

quarry road

4

rocky knoll

Jobson Close

3

quarry

Rydal Cave

Heron Island

2

spoil

shingle

Loughrigg Fell

ants' nest

alder

Rydal Water

5

butterwort

1

White Moss Car Parks

🅿 🆆🅲

Start/ Finish

ice-polished rock

ford

large beech

A591 Grasmere

0   200   400

Metres

RYDAL SITE SUMMARY

1. **Isolated boulder (NY350059)**
   Volcanic rock moved by ice. Stonecrop growing in cracks. Drill-holes provide evidence of blasting.

2. **Rydal Cave (NY355058)**
   Large quarry cave with deep pool full of fish.

3. **Corner of quarry road (NY356058)**
   Oak built into wall. Unusual position of old ash tree indicates that the quarry road redirected the stream.

4. **Small rock at side of path (NY359060)**
   Yellow lichen indicates nitrogen left by perching birds and visiting dogs. A colony of yellow meadow ants hidden underneath.

5. **Marshy area (NY352059)**
   Plants adapted to water-logged, acid soil: home of the yellow-flowering bog asphodel or 'bone breaker'.

use as building material. Look also for a small, succulent plant with white star-shaped flowers. This is English stonecrop, clinging to the dry surface of cracks and crevices. If you climb up onto the top, you will find patches of mustard-coloured lichen showing where birds have regularly landed.

There is a much smaller rock just to the side of this boulder and this also shows the effects of bird-droppings. It is covered in a grey, leafy lichen called crottle but just here its leaves have produced a dusky-red pigment in response to the change in nitrogen levels.

Rejoin the main path, crossing a stream that runs down into a wooded area below. On reaching a second stream, there is a group of insect-eating **butterwort**, arranged like green starfish along the damp ground. Their in-rolled leaves are flooded in sticky fluid and capable of dissolving a fly within hours. After crossing the stream, a path branches off on the right. Do not take this route but keep straight ahead. In the middle of the path look for a smooth, banded rock – shaped like a slice of a barrel. Underneath is a nest of meadow **ants**.

The path now climbs gently past a wooden memorial seat until you reach **Rydal Cave** (**site 2**). Before entering the cave examine the large pile of **spoil** spread out below the path. Its well-drained surface is colonised with stonecrop. Normally this plant would cling to the surface rocks but here in these sheltered conditions its stems are growing upright, some reaching the dizzy height of 4in/13cm!

The quarry cave is a well-known local landmark, but its size is still a surprise. To get inside you need to cross a series of stepping-stones over a deep pool full of fish. Just above the water on a vertical rock face is a patch of 'green' algae that has developed a red pigment. Green algae turn red in bright sunlight. Here, the reflection of the pool's surface doubles the amount of light reaching this south-facing wall.

To continue, cross the stream that leaves the pool and follow the path as it swings down left below the heap of spoil. The path then turns right alongside a fence, passing a group of mature larch before reaching the entrance to a second **quarry**.

Although not as well known as the larger Rydal Cave, this quarry is just as interesting with two cave entrances. The path into it drops steeply down some earth steps with exposed tree roots underneath a sprawling elm. In this sunken hollow, in front of the right-hand entrance, there is wood sorrel, wild geranium and golden saxifrage. But the eye is drawn to the luxuriant ferns that grow characteristically from tight, compact centres. They are known by the rather unflattering name: 'scaly male fern'.

The second cave is further to the left and at a height that is difficult to enter. The rock on the left of the opening shows an interesting section of curved bedding with a drill-hole across its surface where the charge was set for blasting.

On returning to the path, notice how wide and well made it has become. This is the quarry road that was used to transport the quarried rock down to Rydal. The section of wire fence that you are following is soon replaced by a stone wall which curves around to the left to cross

Inside Rydal cave

a stream (**site 3**). As you reach the corner, notice the large oak on the left of the path. Its branches support fine growths of polypody fern 16ft/5m up from the ground.

The wall is unusual. It has been built so that it butts up to the oak with two neatly finished stone edges perfectly matching the shape of the trunk. Follow the wall as it curves left across the stream. The water runs under the **quarry road** and emerges from a square hole in the base of the wall. There is another large tree here which catches the eye. In the bed of the stream is a mature ash. You might expect an alder or a willow to have its feet in water but an ash usually grows in deep, rich soils some distance up from the water's edge. Here it stands in water.

Look at the base of its trunk. There is a bare strip with no moss, lichen or algae. Nothing grows in this narrow band due to the fluctuating water-level. How could such a tree seed itself and take root in the middle of a stream that is regularly flushed through with fast-flowing water? The stream has in fact been redirected during the building of the quarry road. It indicates the amount of earth that was moved at this corner to create a gently sloping route suitable for quarry ponies. Further along, as you follow the 'road' with its accompanying

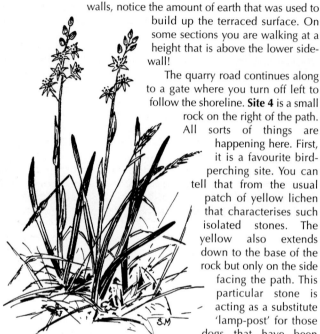

walls, notice the amount of earth that was used to build up the terraced surface. On some sections you are walking at a height that is above the lower side-wall!

The quarry road continues along to a gate where you turn off left to follow the shoreline. **Site 4** is a small rock on the right of the path. All sorts of things are happening here. First, it is a favourite bird-perching site. You can tell that from the usual patch of yellow lichen that characterises such isolated stones. The yellow also extends down to the base of the rock but only on the side facing the path. This particular stone is acting as a substitute 'lamp-post' for those dogs that have been brought this way for a walk. Look closely at the ground under the warm south-facing side. The brown sandy soil is from an ants' nest. Perhaps these meadow ants favour such positions under stones. As well as offering protection from hungry woodpeckers, the rock acts as a solar panel and heat store.

Bog asphodel growing above the shore of Rydal Water

The path continues along the shore of **Rydal Water**. It is broad and level with the exception of a short section that skirts around the **rocky knoll** below Jobson Close. Where the path crosses a ford, have a look at the broad line of **shingle** along the water's edge. On this strandline in summer you will find water mint (purple flowers), tormentil (yellow flowers) and meadowsweet (clusters of small white flowers).

The path is now joined by a wall on the right. There is a slate sign that reads 'White Moss, Grasmere, Red Bank'. About 65ft/20m along from the sign, look for an extensive patch of cup lichen growing up the side of the wall. Continue along the path crossing a small stream with **alder** growing at its edge. A few metres further you reach another stream issuing from the base of a wall (**site 5**). In this marshy area there are a number of interesting plants that have adapted to living with their roots in water. One of these is a certain type of heather, its leaves arranged in groups of four, giving it the name 'cross-leaved heath'. This is the only local heather that can tolerate the high levels of iron found in such water-logged soil.

In late summer, this damp area of marsh will have the yellow star-shaped flowers of bog asphodel (*Narthicium ossifragum*). Quite often in the past, cattle were found with fractured limbs alongside these flowers. The plant was known as the 'bone-breaker' and even today it is called by the scientific name *ossifragum*. How did it get such a repu-tation? The reason links the plant with peaty water. The boat-shaped seeds float on the surface and often beach themselves and take root at the edges of deep marshy pools – the most likely place for a cow to get stuck. In the past, cattle that grazed on this type of acid moorland would lack calcium in their diet and develop weak bones. Bog asphodel just happens to be one of the few eye-catching plants that grow on calcium-deficient soil. The yellow flower certainly got itself noticed, and the 'bone-breaker' got its name.

The rest of the walk is a pleasant stroll alongside the wall to the gate leading back into the wood. From there simply retrace your steps to the starting-point at White Moss car park.

Walk 18

STOCK GHYLL FORCE

*Within half a mile of Ambleside's centre there is a Victorian park.
In 1890 you would have had to pay an entrance fee of threepence
which was increased to sixpence by the early-1900s. After many
years of legal wrangling and court cases involving the townsfolk
and landowner at the time, free access was eventually restored.*

*Stock Ghyll Wood is now a Site of Special Scientific Interest
(SSSI) and it is possibly the best location in Cumbria to find the
rare 'touch-me-not' balsam and the equally rare netted carpet
moth. This moth is found only in the Lake District and the larvae
feed only on the yellow-flowering balsam.*

*On a sunny day this is the place to shelter from the heat
and escape the traffic of Ambleside's busy streets. On a rainy day
it is a welcome outdoor alternative to the shops and cafes... and
it's free!*

THE ROUTE

Stock Ghyll Park is traditionally reached by following the road from
the back of the Salutation Hotel. The entrance has a gate with iron railings. As you follow the wide, shaded path along the south bank of the
river, notice the buildings on the opposite side. They are positioned
alongside a **weir** that was once the site of a **bobbin-mill** driven by a
large water-wheel. But the water supply was not always reliable and
the owner resorted to steam power:

*'The ugly, tall chimney behind [the water-wheel] is a memorial of
the drought of 1859. The owner of the mill suffered so severely
from want of water to carry on his trade, that he determined no
other summer should find him unprepared with a more reliable
power.'* (Guide to the Lake District of England *by Herman Prior,
7th ed, 1890).*

CHECKLIST

Distance:	0.75 mile/1.2km.
Ascent:	200ft/60m.
Approximate Time:	45 minutes.
Maps:	1:25 000 OS Outdoor Leisure 7, The English Lakes, South Eastern area.
Terrain:	Well-maintained footpaths with some steps.
Degree of Shelter:	Extremely sheltered throughout the entire walk.
Stiles:	None.
Special Considerations:	Please do not pick any of the wild flowers or lichens. If you want a record, take a photo.
Footwear:	Walking shoes or trainers.
Parking:	Ample parking space in Ambleside.
Public Transport:	Ambleside is well served with buses from all the other main Lakeland centres.

After approximately 200ft/60m, the path takes you over a small stream. Where the path forks, keep right until you reach a narrow, stone bridge clad in ivy. The path now makes its way between some mature oaks towards a Victorian viewing platform (**site 1**). Notice the iron railings that have been so carefully constructed complete with overhead arches. Today such artificial restraints may seem strange but during the early 1900s when the Lakes were becoming popular, they were thought essential for the safety of tourists and especially for those '*enthusiasts with the camera*', who are warned not to climb over '*lest they get into trouble, as one at least of the fraternity once did*' (The English Lake District by M J B Baddeley, 13th ed).

Return to the main path. In summer this area is dark because of the surrounding beech trees. Ahead of you is another section of iron railing. It is anchored to the trunk of an oak tree (**site 2**). Three bars of iron have been embedded into the trunk. The tree has responded by producing extra layers of cells under its surface and the result is a

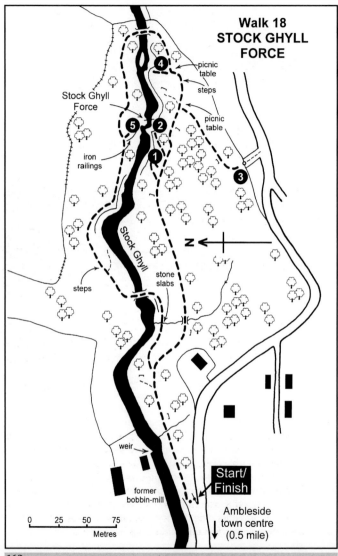

**Walk 18
STOCK GHYLL
FORCE**

Stock Ghyll
Force

picnic
table

steps

picnic
table

iron
railings

Stock Ghyll

stone
slabs

steps

N

weir

Start/
Finish

former
bobbin-mill

Ambleside
town centre
(0.5 mile)

0   25   50   75
Metres

STOCK GHYLL FORCE
SITE SUMMARY

1. **Viewing platform (NY383046)**
    View of falls with elaborate iron railings and arches.

2. **Oak tree (NY383046)**
    Three iron bars embedded in tree trunk causing unusual growth in the tree's outer layers.

3. **Iron turnstile (NY383045)**
    Exit to woodland. Entry was restricted to the lower gate where Victorian tourists were charged an admission fee.

4. **Bank of vegetation (NY384046)**
    Growths of 'dog lichen' – once used as an attempted cure for rabies.

5. **North-bank viewpoint (NY383046)**
    Good view of Stock Ghyll Force. Samples of 'hard fern' with upright, fertile leaves growing alongside path.

strange bond of metal and wood like three swollen knuckles. The oak is producing tannic acid which is slowly dissolving the iron at the junction. (Incidentally, this is why oak furniture is usually made with brass fittings rather than iron which would corrode away.)

Continue climbing the path until you reach a junction in front of a **picnic table**. Take the path to the right which leads to the upper exit fitted with an elaborate iron turnstile (**site 3**). Take a closer look at the top of the wall on either side. It is covered in polypody, a fern that is usually found growing high up on the branches of trees.

The approach to the falls, from a photograph dated between 1878 and 1889, before the introduction of an admission fee (© Armitt Trust)

On retracing your steps back to the junction, you pass an old wooden seat on the left. There are many seats within this woodland. All of them were positioned looking out over a particularly good view, and this seat was no exception – only the wood has since grown and the view from here has long gone.

On returning to the junction, turn right up a series of **steps**. The pink flower growing over the log to the right of the steps is a wild form of geranium called 'herb robert'. At another **picnic table** the path forks. Take the left-hand branch. From the end of this path, carefully retrace your steps counting 20ft/6m back from the railings. Look carefully on the earth bank to your left. This is **site 4** and may require some patient searching. Here you will find a plant that has no flowers. It is called 'dog lichen'. There are nine species of this lichen in Britain. This one has grey-black discs projecting horizontally on top of the leaf (*Peltigera*

Netted carpet moth on touch-me-not balsam

S.M

horizontalis). Dog lichens were once used as an attempted cure for rabies, specifically because the underside of these plants resembles dogs' teeth. The belief was that if it looked like a dog's tooth, it would cure the effects of a dog's tooth – a dog-bite!

Return to the main path which takes you over a wooden footbridge onto the north bank of the river. Follow the path as it drops steadily and look for a small side-path that curves back towards the river to the viewpoint at **site 5**. This is arguably the best view of **Stock Ghyll Force**. (You may have noticed the variation in spelling of Stock Ghyll: whenever the word 'ghyll' is used instead of 'gill', it has usually been retained as a carry-over from Victorian times, indicating its popularity with tourists of that period.) The height of the fall is officially 60ft/18m although 100ft/30m has been quoted in some earlier guides.

As you return to the main path, notice the bank of vegetation on the right. Here are a number of leaves that look like the backbones of fish. These are the fertile leaves of a fern called 'hard fern'. If you look on the back of the leaf in summer, it will have rows of spores. The leaves lying flat against the ground belong to the same plant but look entirely different and produce no spores.

Continue following the main path along the north bank. After descending a series of **steps**, you cross a wooden footbridge and then some **stone slabs** before returning to the path that takes you back to the starting-point.

Walk 19

KENTMERE

There is something strange about the shape of Kentmere Tarn. Most Lakeland valleys were formed by glacial action leaving a symmetrical lake in a scooped-out hollow. The term 'ribbon lake' is often used to describe the long thin outline with parallel sides. But Kentmere Tarn looks more like a ribbon with a knot tied in it.

It wasn't always so. Up until the 1830s 'Kentmere', as it was known, could have been mistaken for a miniature Coniston Water. And then in 1840 it was drained in the hope of providing new land for farming. The result was an acid marshland.

The reason for the poor drainage was a layer of silica-rich plants called diatoms whose remains formed a continuous layer across the valley bottom. When the economic value of this material was realised, it was extracted by dredging the land and a new tarn was formed. Today, the diatomite industry has gone leaving this quiet stretch of water to the local swans and the occasional fisherman.

THE ROUTE

This walk begins and ends at **Kentmere Church**. Follow the farm road heading west towards Kentmere Hall. The road drops gently until you reach an **elder** tree on your left. You are now standing on the shoreline of what used to be the 'mere' of Kentmere. The flat land that you see over the wall on your left was covered in water before it was drained in 1840. The shore followed the 158m contour-line which is roughly the course of the farm road you are now walking.

After passing the elder tree, look out for an unusual mixture of national plants: Scottish harebells on the right and Welsh poppies on the left. You are now in a slight hollow which acts as a frost pocket. Just before the road bends slightly right, it crosses a field drain (**site 1**). This insignificant-looking water-channel used to be the main inlet for water entering the mere. In order to get the full picture we need to go

CHECKLIST

Distance:	4.9 miles/7.8km.
Ascent:	525ft/160m.
Approximate Time:	4 to 5 hours.
Maps:	1:25 000 OS Outdoor Leisure 7, The English Lakes, South Eastern area.
Terrain:	Fairly level well-defined paths for most of the way except for the moorland section between sites 6 and 7 which is boggy and ill-defined in places.
Degree of Shelter:	Very sheltered along the woodland sections but exposed on the moorland alongside Park Beck across to Whiteside End.
Stiles:	One (optional, alongside gate).
Special Considerations:	Navigating the moorland section alongside Park Beck can be difficult in mist.
Footwear:	Boots.
Parking:	There is limited parking space for six or seven cars outside the Church Hall (SD456041).
Public Transport:	Bus services have been intermittent over past years. Check with Stagecoach for details (telephone 0870 608 2608).

back to a time of former global warming, about 5500–3000 BC, just after the last Ice Age but before the main deposits of peat were laid down.

At that time there were two lakes in the valley: the lower one occupying the land over the wall to your left; the upper one out of sight to the right, midway between here and the Kentmere Head Reservoir. The shore of this 'forgotten lake' followed the 226m contour-line and was as large as Buttermere.

What happened to this lake? It used to drain quietly through the gap between Rook Howe and Raven Crag (see OS Outdoor Leisure 7) following the line of the drain in front of you. But there was a second

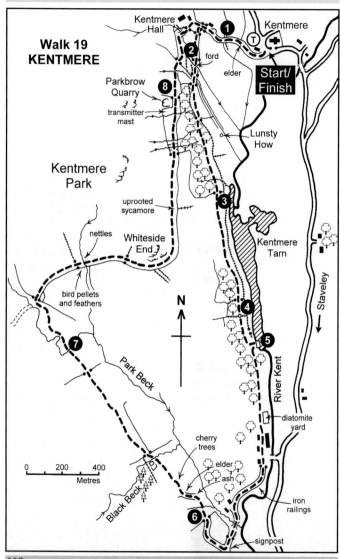

**Walk 19
KENTMERE**

Kentmere Hall

Kentmere

T

Start/
Finish

ford

elder

②

①

Parkbrow
Quarry

⑧

transmitter
mast

Lunsty
How

Kentmere
Park

uprooted
sycamore

③

Kentmere
Tarn

nettles

Whiteside
End

④

bird pellets
and feathers

⑤

Staveley

N

⑦

Park Beck

River Kent

diatomite
yard

0   200   400
Metres

cherry
trees

elder
ash

iron
railings

Black Beck

⑥

signpost

KENTMERE
SITE SUMMARY

1. **Field drain (SD454042)**
   Course of water-channel connecting Kentmere's
   two former lakes.

2. **Fenced plantation (SD452041)**
   Extensive area of meadowsweet along the water's
   edge.

3. **Isolated boulder (SD454033)**
   Lookout perch for ravens. Zones of lichen
   indicating effect of nitrogen from bird-droppings.

4. **Former Kentmere shoreline (SD455027)**
   Old, coppiced ash with dog lichens.

5. **Dredging platform (SD455025)**
   Site of aerial ropeway for removing diatomite.

6. **Isolated boulder (SD453016)**
   Lookout perch for rooks and rubbing-post for
   Highland cattle.

7. **Stepping-stones (SD445025)**
   Water-logged peat deposits with cross-leaved
   heath.

8. **Steep bank (SD451038)**
   Rushes with large population of spiders.

outflow at its south-east corner and this eventually cut through a soft dam of loose moraine. The increased water-flow of this emerging river (the River Kent) continued cutting through the underlying rock creating a much lower outlet at the Force Jump waterfall (north-east of the church) and the lake above simply drained away.

It is interesting to note that during its existence, the upper lake acted as a filter-bed for the lower lake and it was this, coupled with the warm climate, that provided perfect conditions for the growth of diatoms in the lake below.

Continue along the road with **Kentmere Hall** now clearly in view. You pass through two gates and then turn left through a gate in the corner of a wooden fence (sign: 'Public Footpath Only. No Bicycles Please'). The path crosses a grassy field with a plantation of trees fenced-off on the right (**site 2**). Here in the summer months you will find clusters of white flowers on long stems growing along the edge of a stream. This is meadowsweet, once used as a cure for headaches. It contains the chemical salicylic acid, more commonly known as aspirin.

Go through another gate following the path across a concrete **ford** and through two more gates. A few hundred metres ahead of you on the left you can see a smooth grassy mound framed between two prominent trees. This is Lunsty Howe which is marked on some maps (as is Whirl Howe in Longsleddale) as though an ancient barrow or tumulus. It is unlikely that this is a burial mound as it is situated below the former shoreline and therefore would have been partly submerged at the time when such mounds were being built.

The path now climbs gently and leads through a gate into Hall Wood containing mostly sycamore with the occasional birch and coppiced hazel. You emerge from the wood through a gate into open grassland. About 330ft/100m further on the left of the path you reach a large boulder (**site 3**). This is a major landmark for the local population of ravens. All the signs of bird activity are here: the mustard-coloured lichen on top, and rock tripe on the vertical surface below. There is also crottle: normally a turquoise lichen tinged with bronze, but here the nitrogen from the ravens is so concentrated, it has changed the lichen's colour, producing patches of dusky-pink pigment. You should also find raven food-pellets, regurgitated in the manner more associated with owls. And like owl-pellets, they will show what the birds have eaten recently. When I was last here in mid-August, they contained seeds of corn and the hard wing-cases of assorted beetles.

The boulder is also of importance to the local sheep population. At the base of its vertical side, the rock has been polished smooth and the ground below worn into a muddy hollow, showing where the sheep have used this sharp corner as a favourite rubbing-post.

The path you are walking on follows the old shoreline. The 'new' shoreline of **Kentmere Tarn** can be clearly seen below. After passing through a gate in a concrete-post fence, you enter an area with scattered hawthorn and hazel. About 160ft/50m past the gate on the left is an old, coppiced ash (**site 4**). You are now just above the level of the old shoreline and this tree would possibly have been part of a coppiced hedge along the water-margin. Look carefully at the horizontal branches that fan out just above ground level. On the right-hand branch are two varieties of dog lichen (*Peltigera canina and P. polydactyla*). Carefully peel back the leafy structures and note the velcro-like white barbs that attach it to the mossy surface (please do not remove). The spores are produced on chestnut-brown crescents at the ends of the leaves. *Polydactyla* means 'many-fingered' and the crescents are like fingernails.

The path continues along the old shoreline. After crossing a stile, the route becomes narrower as you enter a more enclosed woodland. You pass a gate on your left and then two more coppiced ash trees with growths of dog lichen, wood sorrel and herb robert growing on their mossy branches.

A few metres further, a path leads off to the left to a concrete platform at the water's edge (**site 5**). This is where the diatomite was lifted out of the water and transported by aerial ropeway. The foundations for the support pylons can still be seen. Along the edge of the concrete platform is a line of iron posts that held a safety chain. The former lake bed was dredged using a drag line to scoop out the diatomite and the shape of the new tarn followed the path of the grab bucket as it was pulled along a line from north to south.

Rejoin the shoreline path and continue until you reach the former **diatomite works**. There are few walks in the Lake District where the atmosphere changes as quickly as this. Suddenly you emerge from woodland into an industrial wasteland. The path runs alongside a huge concrete yard enclosed by a 10ft/3m high retaining wall made of railway sleepers. This is the terminus for the aerial ropeway where the dredged sludge was dumped and left to drain before being 'calcined' in a kiln. As recently as the 1970s this yard would have been completely filled with grey earth ready for processing into diatomite. Production continued until 1985.

Kentmere was one of the few sites in Britain where diatomite was worked commercially (the other main centre of production was the Isle of Skye in the early 1900s). Over 70 different species of microscopic diatom have been found in British deposits and when processed they can contain up to 98 per cent silica. Diatomite (or *Kieselguhr*) was added to nitroglycerine to make it safer by absorbing the unstable liquid and transforming it into dynamite. It was also used as an abrasive in the manufacture of toothpaste.

For the biologist there is little to be found on this site except to note the extraordinary growth of cup lichen on the sides of the old sleeper walls. What is interesting is that these lichens are extremely healthy despite growing on wood that was once treated with creosote. Perhaps decades of contact with absorbent silica has removed the toxic creosote from the wood surface.

The path now takes you through a modern factory complex. After leaving the works entrance, look for a gate with a sign: 'Kentmere Pottery', leading along a narrow side-road. The pottery is situated at Sawmill Cottage. Look for a millstone with the date AD 1722 carved on it. Between here and Staveley there were at least 10 water-mills taking power from the River Kent. After the mere was drained in 1840, the flow of river water supplying the mills became so erratic that in 1848 a reservoir was built at Kentmere Head in order to stabilise the flow.

After passing the pottery buildings keep left following the narrow path with **iron railings** on each side. This takes you between some well-kept gardens to a footbridge. Cross the bridge and turn right at the next junction (**signpost**: 'Public Bridleway Kentmere Hall 2.5 miles').

The path climbs gently, enclosed by walls on each side. In August and September there are some excellent wild blackberries to be found along the left-hand side.

A gate leads into the open fellside with a large sweet chestnut tree growing alongside the wall on the left. About 160ft/50m ahead on the left of the path you pass a small ant-hill (home of the yellow meadow ant, *Lasius flavus*). A few metres further above the path is a large isolated boulder (**site 6**). This is almost the same situation found at site 2 where a particular rock takes on great significance for the local birdlife and farm animals. All the signs are here: the yellow lichen on

'...on the skyline above stood the culprit – a Highland cow'

top; the bird-droppings and food-pellets – and the polished surface used as a rubbing-post, except that the corner used here is 3ft/1m above the ground and too high for the sheep. Look carefully at this corner that faces the path. The last time I was here I found traces of ginger hair sticking to it... and on the skyline above stood the culprits: a fold of Highland cattle.

The route now follows a sunken pathway leading gently uphill, bearing left at an old **ash** and then right after passing an **elder** infected with bracket fungus. This particular fungus is called Jew's Ear (*Auricularia auricula-judae*) because of its ear-like shape and because it invariably grows on elder, the tree on which Judas Iscariot was thought to have been hanged.

The path continues to climb gently. Notice the large number of ant-hills on each side where sections of stone wall have been grassed over and the ground is well drained. On the skyline up ahead on the right are three **cherry trees** growing as though planted in a row. The middle one is dead but still standing. The path then drops down past a deserted cottage and walled garden before crossing the ford at **Black Beck**.

Once over the beck, continue through the gate following the grassy path as it climbs steadily with bracken on each side. If the weather is clear, there are good views behind down the Kent Valley with Williamson's Monument prominent on the right. The section ahead is undulating and boggy in places especially after crossing the stepping-stones over Park Beck (**site 7**). The heather growing alongside the path is cross-leaved heath (*Erica tetralix*) and is able to tolerate the water-logged conditions. Its mauve flowers develop in midsummer and the more sunlight the petals receive, the darker they become. Look on the shaded underside of each flower and you will see that it is much paler than the surface exposed to light.

After a short climb, the path drops down once again towards the winding tributary of Park Beck. Do not cross over. Instead, follow the path through a gate and climb gently keeping closely to the left side of a wall that will lead all the way back to Kentmere Hall. This wall is a major landmark. It is part of the ancient boundary wall of Kentmere Park, thought to have been enclosed in the 16th Century. On its up-and-down course, each time it reaches a high point, it becomes a favourite landing place for rooks and crows. On the highest sections, especially where the top is free of any projecting fence wire, you will find **bird-pellets** and crows' **feathers** and as well as the familiar tinge of yellow.

One other notable feature on this section is a large patch of **nettles** alongside a small stream that crosses the path. The stream drains a large catchment area that is kept well fertilised for growing silage. The nettles indicate the high levels of nitrogen that have run off from the ground above.

After contouring around the crags of **Whiteside End**, the path begins to drop steadily. Look for an old **sycamore** that has been uprooted and left alongside the wall. It is covered in a brightly coloured bracket fungus that resembles oyster shells (*Trametes versicolor*).

After passing through a complicated series of gates and sheep-pens, the path drops more steeply past a **transmitter mast** and the disused **Parkbrow Quarry**. Some of the blue slate gravestones outside Kentmere Church came from here. The slate is also to be found in the walls bordering the path up ahead. Notice the fine growths of maidenhair spleenwort found growing almost exclusively on the shaded north-east-facing sides.

Once you have passed the next gate, there is an interesting grass-covered bank rising steeply to your left (**site 8**). The slope is covered in the spiky stems of the soft rush, *Juncus effusus*. If you are passing here before midday and the ground is damp from dew, mist or rain, look up the bank towards the sun. Strung out across the tops of the rushes are thousands of spiders' webs. Normally they would go unnoticed but the drops of water, the angle of slope and the backlighting bring them all into full view.

A little further down, in the middle of the path, are two plants often found where the ground is well trampled. Try spotting marsh cudweed covered in white downy hairs and pineapple mayweed that actually smells of pineapple when its flowers are crushed.

Just before crossing a small stream, you pass a large alder tree on the left and then a strange-looking ash over the wall on the right. The ash has had its top sawn off and just below the cut surface is a clump of soft rush that is managing to grow in a wet hollow 10ft/3m above the ground.

As the path drops down through the next gate, there is a fine view of Kentmere Hall with its 14th Century pele tower. Down to the right of the path, you pass a large sycamore. This is a most accommodating tree. Notice the young rowan that has taken root in its branches and the rooks nesting up above. Scattered around its base there are mole-hills.

The path takes you across a low, concrete footbridge. A few metres past the bridge on the left over a wire fence is a tree sometimes mistaken for a sycamore. Its more compact leaves are those of the field maple (*Acer campestre*) – the only true British maple.

You are now back at the farm road outside **Kentmere Hall**. Retrace your steps back to the church. If you have time, it is worthwhile visiting the churchyard to see the yew tree. This fine tree has two trunks held together with an iron chain. One of the trunks is now dead but still acts as a support for the other. Its girth has been measured at 15ft/4.5m which would suggest an age of up to 600 years.

Walk 20

CUNSWICK SCAR

Many visitors intent on walking the Lakeland hills will pass through Kendal without thinking of walking the Kendal hills, leaving this outlying countryside for the locals to enjoy. The area does not form part of any long-distance footpath. Neither does it form any direct walking link with the rest of Lakeland. Scars are often isolated by farmland and their linear nature means that they do not have walks developed as 'Horseshoes' or 'Rounds'.

Walking on limestone offers an alternative experience. Most of the scars on the south-east edge of the Lake District are SSSIs and none is more easily accessible than Cunswick Scar. Here is a complete contrast to the Central Fells and a chance to see why such outlying areas have been labelled 'Sites of Special Scientific Interest'.

THE ROUTE

This walk starts at the car park between Scout Scar and Cunswick Scar on the Underbarrow Road. The first thing to notice if the weather is wet is the slipperiness of the car park surface. This is a limestone pavement and rainwater is continuously dissolving its surface leaving a thin film of calcium and magnesium salts which acts as a lubricant.

From the **car park**, take the path through an ash and hazel wood that leads past the **transmitter mast** to a gate (signpost: 'Permitted Path Cunswick Fell'). The path follows the wall around the edge of a field, passing another signpost. The limestone pavement is never far below the surface and is exposed in certain places. This type of grassland is one of the richest in the area for its variety of wild flowers. Look for wild thyme, harebell and spear thistle amongst the grass, and herb robert on the stone outcrops.

Scattered around the field are hawthorns that have been grazed by cattle. Grazing encourages side-shoots to form. The trees are no more than columns of short twigs, some of which are less than 3ft/1m high!

CHECKLIST

Distance:	3.6 miles/5.8km.
Ascent:	360ft/110m.
Approximate Time:	2 to 3 hours.
Maps:	1:25 000 OS Outdoor Leisure 7, The English Lakes, South Eastern area.
Terrain:	Mostly dry lanes and footpaths. Level, well-drained grassland on top of scar.
Degree of Shelter:	Sheltered along the lower woodland sections.
Stiles:	Four.
Special Considerations:	Please keep to the public footpaths when passing Cunswick Hall.
Footwear:	Boots.
Parking:	Public car park at the top of Underbarrow Road (SD489924).
Public Transport:	Regular bus services supply Kendal (2 miles/3km from Underbarrow Road car park).

As you follow the wall, and just before the overhead electric wire crosses it, you reach a group of trees growing against the wallside. You pass an elder, a yew and then an ash. A few metres further and the path goes alongside an outcrop of limestone pavement (**site 1**). Look carefully around the rock margins for the yellow flowers of lady's bedstraw and the white, compact florets of yarrow. When I was last here, one of these rocks had been used as a thrush's anvil with fragments of snail shells scattered over its flat surface. This particular snail, *Cepaea*, has alternate brown and yellow bands and is commonly found in limestone areas. The occurrence of snails reflects the soil's chemistry: snails need calcium to make a shell.

Follow the wall past more grazed hawthorn until you reach **Gamblesmire Lane** and turn left through the gate. Notice the large oak about 100ft/30m along the lane on the left. Its lower leaves have all been grazed to the same height above the ground.

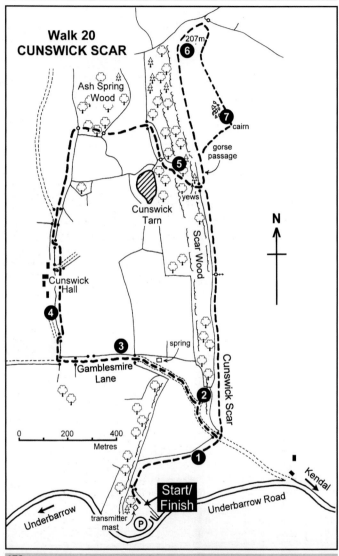

**Walk 20
CUNSWICK SCAR**

Ash Spring Wood

207m

6

7 cairn

gorse passage

5

yews

Cunswick Tarn

Scar Wood

N

Cunswick Hall

4

spring

3

Gamblesmire Lane

2

0   200   400
Metres

Cunswick Scar

1

Start/ Finish

Kendal

Underbarrow Road

Underbarrow

transmitter mast

P

CUNSWICK SCAR
SITE SUMMARY

1. **Limestone outcrop (SD492927)**
   Thrush's anvil with lady's bedstraw and yarrow.

2. **Limekiln (SD492929)**
   Well-preserved example with Romanesque arch.
   Spleenwort growing on the underside.

3. **A lichen puzzle (SD488931)**
   Does the type of tree and the prevailing wind
   direction affect the plant growth on this stone
   wall?

4. **Group of dead trees (SD486932)**
   Interesting radiating pattern left by wood-boring
   beetle under bark.

5. **Scar Wood (SD491938)**
   Quiet woodland with ash, sycamore and yew. The
   field layer includes wild strawberry and hart's-
   tongue fern.

6. **Viewpoint (SD491943)**
   Extensive views from top of scar over Kentmere
   and south-east Lakeland.

7. **Limestone scree (SD492939)**
   Loose rocks containing fossils of solitary corals.

The limekiln at site 2 – a good place to shelter in heavy rain.

The lane descends between scattered hawthorn and ash and then a right-hand fork leads down to a limekiln (**site 2**). Such kilns are found in large numbers in limestone regions on both sides of the Pennines. Over 270 kilns have been recorded recently in the parishes of Sedbergh, Garsdale and Dent.

The front chamber has a Romanesque arch and a magnificent barrel-vaulted ceiling (notice the fine growths of maiden-hair spleen-wort). This is a good place to shelter in heavy rain.

Most of these square kilns were built in the early 1800s. Hidden within the square structure is a 'pot' about 6.5ft/2m in diameter and 10ft/3m deep, shaped like an egg-cup with a draw-hole at the bottom. The pot was filled with alternate layers of limestone and fuel which was lit from below. The fire would burn slowly for three or four days, converting the limestone to quicklime. Temperatures inside would reach 1000 degrees C which meant that the firing-chamber of unlined kilns frequently crumbled and had to be rebuilt.

Retrace your steps back to the path junction and continue along the lane. After passing through a gate, the track follows a field wall (**site 3**). On your right there is a single oak and then a row of nine sycamores – and this presents us with a puzzle. Take a close look at the wall. It has a bright yellow lichen growing on some sections but not on others. The lichen's name is *Xanthoria* from the Greek word for yellow. That's the easy bit! The puzzle is: why does it grow under the oak and not under any of the ash? Even more puzzling is why does it start underneath the mid-point of the oak and extend along the wall several metres beyond the overhanging branches on its east side? That's the puzzle. It may be significant that the prevailing wind comes from the west... and then westerly winds usually bring rain whilst easterlies are mostly dry. Or perhaps oak is preferred to ash as a suitable roosting site.

At the end of the row of trees, turn right to follow the field wall. A signpost ('Public Footpath') indicates the way through a gate and the path continues with the wall now on your left. After several metres you come to a section of broken wall with various dead trees behind it (**site 4**). Notice how one of these dead trees (behind an elder) has been attacked by a bark beetle, leaving an elaborate pattern of radiating channels.

The path now goes alongside some farm buildings until you reach a gate leading onto a muddy farm track. Do not turn left (this leads to **Cunswick Hall**). Keep straight ahead with the wall on your left for 200ft/60m and then a gate leads out of the field and onto the farm road.

The path follows the field wall on your right, crosses a cattle grid and then passes through a gate in an electric fence. After 980ft/300m, turn right at a yellow waymark, through a gap-stile into **Ash Spring Wood**. This dark wood is mostly sycamore and beech. The path leads to a second gap-stile taking you out of the wood and into a field. On my last visit here, this field was full of young partridges that followed me around, expecting to be fed!

There is no clear path across this field but make your way to a gate in the wire fence that encloses the woodland opposite. Once through the gate the path follows another fence with woodland on the left and open marsh on the right. After crossing a stile, the path forks. Take the left-hand path that climbs up between the ash and hazel.

This is a magnificent limestone scar wood (**site 5**) that is hardly visited even in the summer. As you climb between the limestone outcrops, you find plants that are refreshingly different from those found in Central Lakeland. Where the path becomes steep, look for

*Juniper berries take two years to mature and change
from green to the more familiar black*

two **yews** on the left and notice how there is very little plantlife growing underneath. Yews produce poisons that effect the soil below and their dense leaves effectively keep out the sunlight. This contrasts with the sycamore growing 16ft/5m further along to the right of the path. Here can be found wild strawberry, herb robert and hart's-tongue fern.

The path now makes its final climb to the top of the scar through parallel bands of limestone and more yew. The top is reached through a gate in a wire fence. The yellow marker points to the right but take the path left along the edge of the scar.

Keep a look-out for scattered bird feathers along this section. This is a favourite haunt of peregrines that take advantage of the open space above the trees to bring down their prey.

The path now goes through a passage lined with **gorse**, bramble and hawthorn: Goretex-wearers beware! Look for a juniper ahead and to the right. It is full of berries, some green and some the more familiar black. Juniper berries take two years to mature and change colour.

The wire fence on the left ends at the edge of the scar. The path continues on a level with the tops of yew, hazel and whitebeam growing on the limestone ledges just below. On a clear day, the walk along the edge of the scar to its north end (**site 6**) provides excellent views across to Kentmere and Longsleddale and the dry, level surface makes for easy walking. Amongst the grass, look for carline thistle and small scabious.

After reaching the north end of the scar, return along the high ground visiting the loose pile of limestone scree scattered below the west-facing slope (**site 7**). Some of these stones contain fossils – mostly solitary corals that once lived in the sea 300 million years ago.

Make your way past the groups of yew and ash to the highest point on the skyline, marked by a small **cairn**. Looking west from here you can just see the outline of Cunswick Tarn over the edge of the scar. From the cairn, drop down to rejoin the path along the edge of the scar. You pass the gate where you first emerged from above the woodland and continue with the fence on your right. The path wanders between gorse and various forms of stunted yew and prostrate juniper. All along this section there are ant-hills built by the yellow meadow ant. Some are 30cm high indicating well-established colonies that are thriving on the well-drained soil.

The path crosses a wire fence over a stile and returns to **Gamblesmire Lane** from where you can retrace your steps back to the car park.

NOTES AND BIBLIOGRAPHY

1. Sale Fell. An account of graptolytes in the Lake District is given in *Lakeland Geology*, E H Shackleton (1969); Dalesman Publications.

If you wish to see specimens of local graptolytes, there is a collection on display at the Keswick Museum and Art Gallery (open Easter to the end of October, 7 days a week, 10am to 4pm).

2. The Glenderaterra Valley. For more information on the geology of this valley, see *Lakeland Rocks and Landscape: A Field Guide*, edited by Mervyn Dodd (1992); Ellenbank Press.

Extensive details of the lead mines can be found in *Mines of the Lake District Fells* by John Adams (1988); Dalesman Publications.

3. Lanthwaite Wood. The green alga at site 2 is *Trentepohlia aurea* growing in a previously unknown gelatinous form. Further details regarding this specimen can be obtained from the British Museum of Natural History, London.

4. Scale Force. For an all-round reference book on fungi (including the 'razor-strop') and other non-flowering plants, see *The Oxford Book of Flowerless Plants*, F H Brightman and B E Nicholson (1966); Oxford University Press.

Reference to the mining activity at Scale Force can be found in *Mines of the Lake District Fells* by John Adams (see above).

5. Johnny Wood and Scaleclose Coppice. The glacial features of Rosthwaite are described in detail in *Lakeland Rocks and Landscape* edited by Mervyn Dodd (see above).

A list of the flora and fauna found in the Borrowdale Woods is given in *A Nature Conservation Revue*, edited by D A Ratcliffe (1977); Cambridge University Press.

The 'witches' brooms' above site 4 are caused by the fungus *Exoascus turgidus*.

The chemistry of mineral and organic soils such as those found at site 5 is explored in *Wetland Ecology: The Institute of Biology's Studies in Biology no. 154*, John R Etherington (1983); Edward Arnold.

6. Watendlath. Research on the cause of the 'oily film' that forms on the surface of peaty water is in progress. Two theories have been suggested: 1) diffraction by a thin, surface-layer of bacteria – mostly *Bacillus subtilis*; 2) diffraction by a thin surface-layer of colloidal iron.

7. High-Level Route (Pillar). *The Wild Flowers of Britain and Northern Europe*, Richard Fitter,

Alastair Fitter, Marjorie Blamey (1974); Collins, is a good pocket-sized field guide to the flowers (including alpines) found on this walk.

The brown sandstone at site 4 is volcanic. The term 'sandstone' refers to the size of the particles from which it is made.

8. Dalegarth. For a photographic guide to many of the ferns and lichens found on this walk, see *Grasses, Ferns, Mosses and Lichens of Great Britain and Ireland*, Roger Phillips (1980); Pan Books.

The variety of lichen found in Dalegarth Wood is unexpectedly less than is found in the Borrowdale Woods. This has been attributed to the difference in management at Dalegarth which was clear-felled in the late 1700s. See *Lichens as Pollution Monitors, The Institute of Biology's Studies in Biology no.66*, David L Hawksworth and Francis Rose (1976); p.21, Edward Arnold.

9. Tilberthwaite Gill. A comprehensive account of the mines of this area is given in *Coniston Copper Mines: A Field Guide to the Copper ore Field at Coniston in the English Lake District*, Eric G Holland (1981); Cicerone Press.

A general introduction to lichens and descriptions of those found on this walk can be found in *The Observer's Book of Lichens*, Kenneth L Alvin (1977); Frederick Warne.

10. Wallowbarrow and Grassguards. For more information on this area see *Walks around Furness and the Duddon*, Ian Brodie (1985); Dalesman Publications.

The 'northern' or 'hairy' wood ant (*F. lugubris*) is also found in Borrowdale around Lodore and Ashness Bridge. In Victorian times, colonies of these ants were often introduced into pheasantries to provide food for the young birds.

11. Aira Force. Information on dimensions of 'champion' trees in Cumbria as well as the rest of the British Isles can be obtained from TROBI (The Tree Register of the British Isles), 77a Hall End, Wooton, Bedfordshire MK43 9HP or e-mail: trobi@aol.com.

12. Moor Divock. Historical evidence for a 'serpentine avenue' linking the archaeological sites is discussed in *From Carnac to Callanish: the Prehistoric Stone Rows and Avenues of Britain, Ireland and Brittany*, Aubrey Burl (1993); Yale University.

There are two theories that explain the formation of shake-holes:
1) the limestone dissolves away underground and the area above catastrophically collapses into it; 2) the surface limestone dissolves away slowly from contact with water at ground level caused by impeded drainage from a raised water-table. On Moor Divock, the second process is more likely – the shake-holes occupying a distinct band where the edge of the limestone overlies impervious volcanic rock.

13. Knipe Scar. Reference to the 'stone avenue' that extends from Shap to Knipe Scar can be found in *From Carnac to Callanish* by Aubrey Burl (see above).

14. Martindale. An excellent history of Martindale and its churches is given in *A Short History of Martindale* by C N Barrand. This is now out of print but a copy may be seen at the Pooley Bridge Tourist Information Centre.

For information on the Martindale Yew see *The Cumbrian Yew Book*, Ken Mills (1999); Yew Trees for the Millennium in Cumbria.

The green alga on and under the yew's branches is *Desmococcus*. It is frequently found in city areas where pollution levels restrict lichen growth.

15. Silver Point. For botanists wishing to check the flora recorded for this area as well as for a systematic account of all the other grid squares in Cumbria, see *The Flora of Cumbria*, Geoffrey Halliday (1997); University of Lancaster, ISBN 1-86220-051-3.

16. Four Stones Hill. For an account of 'pollen analysis' and its use in recording the changes in climate in the Lake District since the last glacial period, see *Mountains and Moorlands*, W H Pearsall (1950); The Fontana New Naturalist.

Reference to the Haweswater Copper Mines can be found in *Mines of the Lake District Fells*, John Adams (1988); Dalesman Publications.

17. Rydal. The fish in Rydal Cave are minnows that were introduced into the pool by the Freshwater Biological Association (Windermere).

18. Stock Ghyll Force. The guidebooks by Herman Prior and M J B Baddeley from which the quotes are taken can be seen in Ambleside's Armitt Museum and Library.

19. Kentmere. For information on the former lakes of the Kentmere valley see *Principles of Physical Geography*, F J Monkhouse (1971); pp.203–205, University of London Press.

A history of the Kentmere valley from the Stone Age to the present can be found in *A Lakeland Valley through Time*, edited by Joe Scott (1995); Staveley and District History Society.

20. Cunswick Scar. A good description of limekilns of the period (similar to the one at site 2) is given in 'Limekilns in Sedbergh, Garsdale and Dent', Ingram Cleasby; *Current Archaeology* 145, pp.16–20.